Artia

JIŘÍ TRNKA

JAROSLAV BOČEK

JIŘÍ
TRNKA

Artist and Puppet Master

ARTIA

Note to the Reader

The name Jiří Trnka is easily pronounced in English
by reading aloud the following spelling:

"Yershy Trinka"

First English edition 1965
English translation by Till Gottheiner
Expert collaboration by Stella Rodway
Graphic design by Antonín Kodeda
Designed and produced by Artia
© Jaroslav Boček 1963
Illustrations © Jiří Trnka 1963
S 1619

In my opinion
Trnka is the pride of the Czech nation.
In my modest opinion
he is the pride of Mankind

NAZIM
HIKMET

CONTENTS

Jiří Trnka, the great Czech puppeteer, is often said to be an innovator, and this is true. His talent is highly original, but he has also introduced a new medium to the cinema: the puppet film. Yet it is true, too, that basically his work can be regarded as a climax, even an epilogue, to the work of the past, which is why it is so mellow and mature. Trnka has not merely inherited the traditions of Czech puppetry: his work actually springs from them. It is the fruit of generations of puppeteers, deriving directly from Czech folk puppetry, the skills of which he has developed to their culminating point, and even exhausted. This helps to explain his special position in contemporary Czech art.

It is only by understanding this position that we can come to understand his work. At a superficial glance he might seem suddenly to have appeared an artist, whose work was unrelated to time or to normal evolution, like a stray boulder in a landscape of utterly different geological composition. But that is to overlook its national character, which is essentially Czech, and also the reflection in it of present-day life. Trnka's position in contemporary Czech art is special in the sense of being outstanding, unique, rather than strange or inexplicable.

It is difficult to write even casually of Trnka without emphasising his unusual personality, but this is something he shares with most people of original talent. And talent, of whatever kind, reaches fulfilment within the boundaries of definite time and place. It is tied to these by a million threads, and they influence it as it takes its ultimate form. Art, in fact, bears witness to its own period and environment.

Trnka's art is no exception. Original though he is, his work is an organic growth, rooted in the history of Bohemia. And its character is such that we cannot imagine it as having flowered anywhere but in the Czechoslovakia of today.

Trnka's first puppets

I

IN A SENSE, it was destiny which led Trnka to the puppet film. The story of his work, as with any artist, had begun long before he came on to the scene. He was the son of Rudolf Trnka, a plumber, and was born on February 24th, 1912, in a suburb of Plzeň (Pilsen), in Bohemia. In his own home circle and outside it, work in puppetry had developed to a stage where it was to exert a decisive influence on a highly impressionable child.

Doll-making was a familiar occupation in the household, and he must have met his first puppet at a very early age. His grandmother, Madlena Rohbergerová, helped the family budget by painting earthenware and also making and selling toy horses and dolls. His mother was a dressmaker, and she made Jiří's first toys from bits of rag. It was not long before the small child was imitating them both and improving upon his own toys, or making new ones.

He was soon to see puppets in action: at the afternoon performances for children at the Holiday Camp Theatre. This theatre had a fine tradition in puppetry, and presented a varied repertory, including opera and light opera, drama, variety shows and revues. It put on works by Offenbach, Mozart and Gluck, Pushkin and Molière as well as the Czech classics.

The Holiday Camp Theatre was run by Josef Skupa, who took it over in 1916, when Trnka was four years old. Seven years later, when Jiří was eleven, he went to the secondary school, where Josef Skupa was working as a young art teacher. Skupa soon noticed the boy's talent and interest in puppetry, and it was not long before Trnka found himself on the other side of the curtain at the Holiday Camp Theatre. To begin with, Skupa allowed Trnka and the other boys to help with odd jobs. Later he gave them more important work. They helped to paint the backcloths, repair broken puppets, even to make simple stage props. Trnka's years of apprenticeship as a puppeteer had begun.

The Holiday Camp Theatre introduced him to both the classics and contemporary work. When Josef Skupa took over in 1916 he began a satirical feature known as Kaspar's Cabaret. Kaspar, played and spoken by Skupa himself, gave a commentary on political life, in the form of jokes, criticism and ridicule. He attacked the monarchy, oppression and war. As early as September 2nd, 1918, over a month before the final

event, he performed the burial rites of the Austro-Hungarian Empire on his stage.

Thus Trnka encountered both traditional and new influences. From the older traditions of the folk puppeteers Trnka learned that the puppet was something other than a mere imitation of a living actor. It was a medium of artistic expression in its own right, with its own special technical and stylistic requirements.

From Josef Skupa Trnka learned that tradition should not be allowed to make an art-form static, and that many of the older traditions of puppetry were out of date, and needed developing and infusing with new life by means of different techniques, a different style of puppet drama, new poetry. He learned that art should go forward, and that there was great scope for originality.

But these influences were absorbed unconsciously. At the time, the boy was merely happy to be taking part in the work of grown-up people, and he was greatly thrilled when the first puppet he designed was used at the theatre by Josef Skupa.

Knight   Clown   Pilgrim and Don Quixote

The Trnka display at the International Puppet Exhibition in Prague, 1929

INEVITABLY, Jiří was paying more attention to the little theatre than to his school work, and in a sense puppetry was unlucky for him at this time. His school reports were not very good, and this influenced the family, who were at a time of crisis, in their decision to take Jiří and his younger brother away from school and set them to earning a living.

The family's circumstances had become serious. When Jiří was in the fourth form at school his father's plumbing business went bankrupt. Rudolf Trnka had been unsettled by several years in the trenches during the First World War, and he had

managed only by a great effort to keep his head above water. Now the family, who had already been living very modestly, were in dire need.

Jiří was apprenticed to a pastry-cook. Geometry, arithmetic, art and technical drawing had to give way to pastry and cream cakes. But within two months Jiří had changed his job. His white overalls were replaced with blue dungarees, and for a short while he learnt the trade of locksmith in the Plzeň Škoda Works. But then Josef Skupa intervened to find him more congenial work, in the arts and crafts shop.

Jiří had not, of course, given up the little theatre. It was inevitable that, at a time when his days were occupied by work that did not

Advertisements for Skupa

interest him, he should have turned more and more towards puppetry. He spent his evenings in concentrated work for the theatre, painting back-cloths, designing stage props, designing, carving, and clothing the puppets themselves. Sporadically at first, his name began to appear on publicity material. As time passed, the last item on the programme would often read: Puppets: Gustav Nosek and Jiří Trnka.

The puppets Trnka made for Skupa's theatre were the usual characters of variety shows: there were puppets with elongated necks, grotesque groups of identical little figures, ballet dancers, circus folk. But these were not the only puppets he was making at that time. He produced others for himself: as a hobby, and as a means of self-expression. These were not meant for the theatre: they were decorative little creatures, almost masks. Trnka had no particular purpose in mind, but these puppets interpreted the impressions made on him by the books he had read, and the characters in them: Don Quixote, Hamlet,

Work at the School of Applied Arts

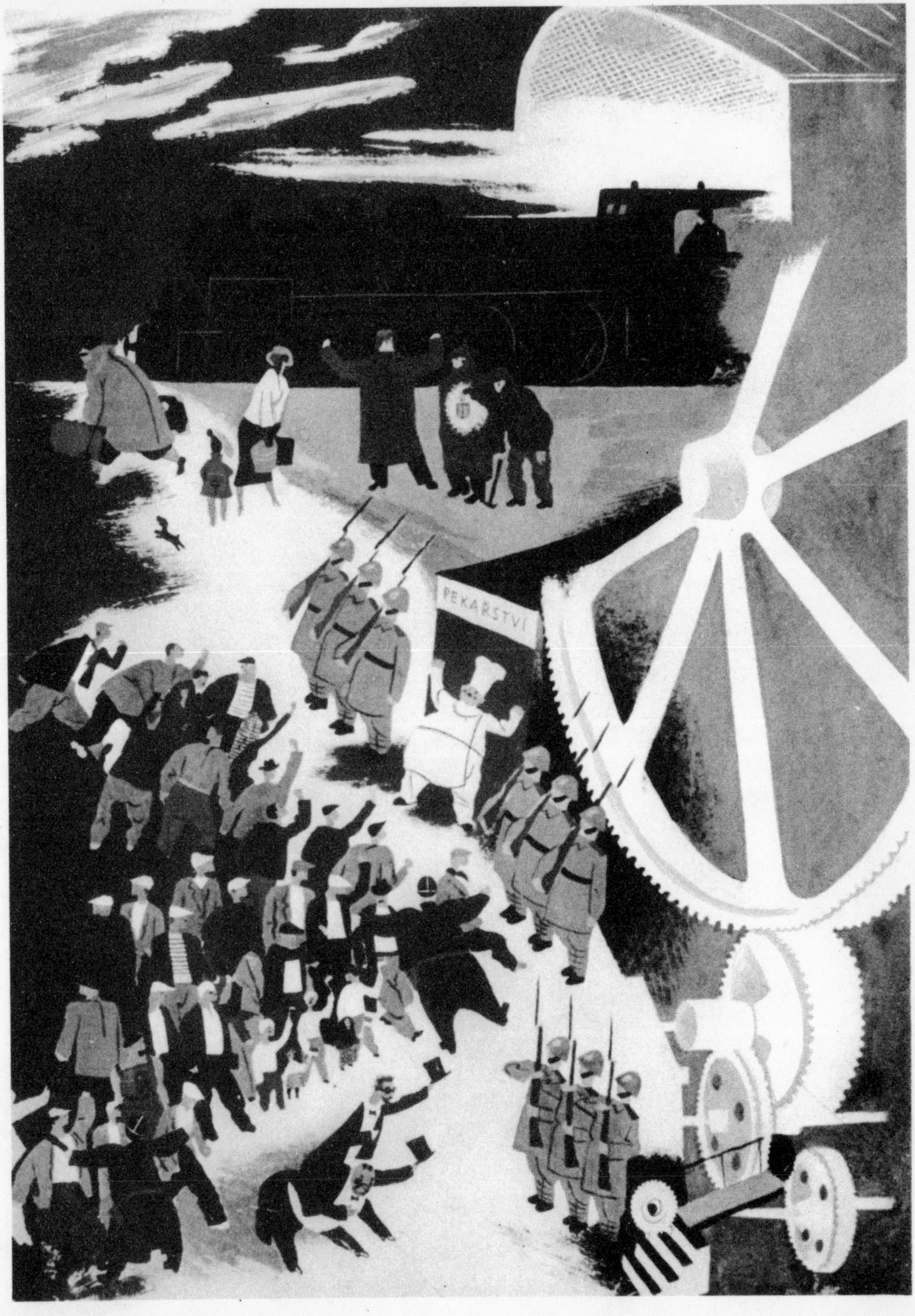

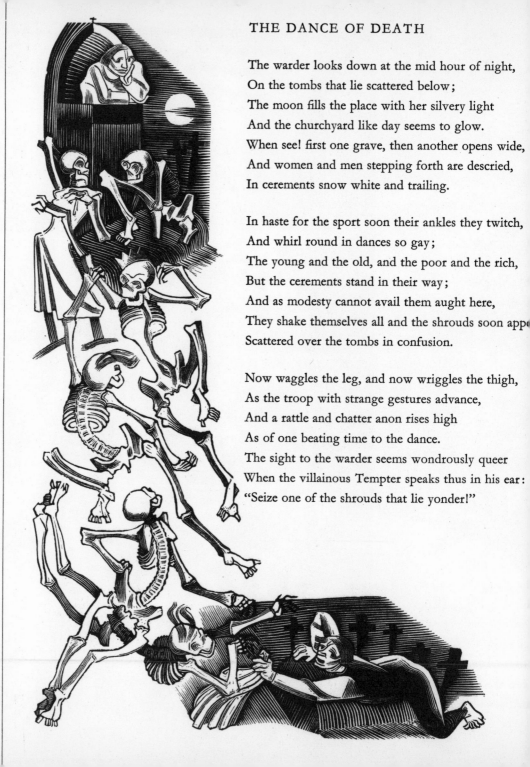

Woodcuts for Goethe's *Totentanz* (Exhibited at Leipzig)

THE DANCE OF DEATH

The warder looks down at the mid hour of night,
On the tombs that lie scattered below;
The moon fills the place with her silvery light
And the churchyard like day seems to glow.
When see! first one grave, then another opens wide,
And women and men stepping forth are descried,
In cerements snow white and trailing.

In haste for the sport soon their ankles they twitch,
And whirl round in dances so gay;
The young and the old, and the poor and the rich,
But the cerements stand in their way;
And as modesty cannot avail them aught here,
They shake themselves all and the shrouds soon appe
Scattered over the tombs in confusion.

Now waggles the leg, and now wriggles the thigh,
As the troop with strange gestures advance,
And a rattle and chatter anon rises high
As of one beating time to the dance.
The sight to the warder seems wondrously queer
When the villainous Tempter speaks thus in his ear:
"Seize one of the shrouds that lie yonder!"

Quick as thought it was done! and for safety he fled
Behind the church door with all speed;
The moon still continues her clear light to shed
On the dance that they fearfully lead.
But the dancers at length disappear one by one,
And their shrouds, ere they vanish, they carefully don,
And under the turf all is quiet.

But one of them stumbles and shuffles there still,
And gropes at the graves in despair;
Yet 'tis by no comrade he's treated so ill;
The shroud he soon scents in the air.
So he rattles the door—for the warder 'tis well
That 'tis bless'd and so able the foe to repel,
All covered with crosses of metal.

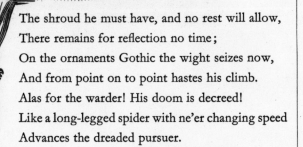

The shroud he must have, and no rest will allow,
There remains for reflection no time;
On the ornaments Gothic the wight seizes now,
And from point on to point hastes his climb.
Alas for the warder! His doom is decreed!
Like a long-legged spider with ne'er changing speed
Advances the dreaded pursuer.

The warder he quakes, and the warder turns pale
The shroud to restore fain had sought;
When the end,—now can nothing to save him avail,
In a tooth formed of iron is caught.
With vanishing lustre the moon's race is run
When the bell thunders loudly a powerful One,
And the skeleton falls, crushed to atoms.

J. W. Goethe

Version by Edgar Alfred Bowring, C. B.

Mercutio. He made them simply because he had the urge to do so.

Trnka's two years earning his own living were not wasted: they were years in the school of life, and they taught him that nothing was to be had without working for it. Talent, he realised, meant very little by itself, unless given its fullest expression through work, carried out with determination and will-power. Nevertheless, the two years confirmed him in his resolve to devote his life to art.

JOSEF SKUPA, who had helped him so far, felt a great responsibility towards his gifted pupil, and was concerned for his future. He felt that the life Jiří was leading did not give him enough opportunity to develop his talent. Skupa was convinced that, in the field of puppetry, a talented person could no longer make his way without a specialist training. He therefore tried to persuade Jiří's family to send him to the School of Applied Arts in Prague. The family hesitated because of the difficulties of providing for the boy, but Skupa put forward a concrete proposal, and then his arguments bore fruit.

In September, Jiří, now sixteen years old, set out for Prague knowing that his needs would be provided for. He stayed at his brother's flat, which did not involve the family in the extra expense of lodgings. His midday meal was provided free by the Bohemian Heart, a charity organisation which catered for poor students. But, while he studied, he still had to earn money to provide for his other needs: his breakfast, supper, clothes and equipment for the school.

He was able to earn from two sources. One was Skupa's theatre, for which Trnka continued to work as a stage and puppet designer. The other was a children's newspaper called *Night Time*. The editor was one of Skupa's collaborators, and gave Jiří work as an illustrator.

The School of Applied Arts came first, of course. It was an art school of the traditional type, where stress was placed heavily on craftsmanship and the complete mastery of technique. Trnka found this especially so in Professor Benda's class in graphic design, which he attended. He became an outstanding student. A design he made in his third year, a carving illustrating Goethe's poem, *The Dance of Death*, was chosen to represent Czech graphic art at a Goethe Exhibition in Leipzig, in 1931.

2

IN JUNE 1935, Trnka graduated from the School of Applied Arts. He was now twenty-three and had to face the vital question of his future career.

He had an income from his newspaper illustrations which more or less covered his current expenses. His work had been accepted by other publishing houses, so that he was no longer dependent on the children's magazine *Night Time*. But he did not feel this to be sufficient, and decided to seek a proper job.

By this time Josef Skupa had left the Holiday Camp Theatre, which, despite its reputation, was really in the strict sense an amateur company. Skupa had turned professional, and had set up his own travelling theatre, with the result that the Holiday Camp Theatre had been closed down. Trnka, acting on the suggestion of one of Skupa's assistants, wrote a revue for its re-opening, which took place in the autumn, with Trnka as director and stage designer.

Trnka's revue was called *The Merman*. It was a grotesque piece following the traditions of Skupa's own revues. It was a parody of the fantastic adventures and exaggerated

From the production
of *The Fireflies*

From the production of *Mr. Eustachius, the Dog and the Sultan*

pathos of sea-faring adventure stories. The stock characters were burlesqued by such figures as Captain Joe Flint, Legless Jack and Wild Sam. The plot was far-fetched and accompanied by continuous back-chat. There was also a musical accompaniment which included parodies of popular songs current at the time, taken from the repertoire of Marlene Dietrich.

The opening night was a success, the reviews were favourable, and, after a number of performances in Plzeň, the company performed *The Merman* in Prague, as guest artists. Again they were successful. Trnka realised all the more forcefully, however, that to return to Plzeň with the Holiday Camp Theatre was no permanent solution for him. It was an amateur company which could at best offer only occasional work. Skupa's other theatre, though it was always travelling about the country, was really based in Plzeň, and the suburb could not support two professional theatres. Trnka therefore rejected a plan to set up a new puppet theatre of his own.

Almost a year passed in part-time activities. Trnka continued to make his own puppets, and he still earned his living doing illustrations for the newspapers, while keeping a look-out for more important work.

Trnka's opportunity came exactly a year after he had graduated: in June 1936. On this date the two-man satirical theatre, the Theatre in Fetters, run by Voskovec and Werich, moved out of the Rococo Hall in Prague. Trnka was able to take it over, and on September 13th of the same year, he opened his Wooden Theatre with a play called *Among the Fireflies*.

TRNKA had great hopes for his theatre, and cherished secret dreams of outshining his teacher, Josef Skupa. His assistants were carefully chosen, and he was lucky in them. The staff numbered twenty-four. But it was Trnka himself who made and clothed the puppets, designed the stage, produced the play and took part in it. He also managed the publicity. Everything was carefully thought out, and Trnka had had several years of experience as a puppeteer. Success seemed assured. The opening performance was free to all school-children in Prague. Trnka was hoping later to give children's matinees several days a week, and to produce plays for adults in the evening.

Among the Fireflies was based upon a currently successful book, and Trnka thought it would be bound to attract attention. But it failed to win the acclaim he had hoped for. For his second play he tried the effect of a publicity stunt. *Basil and the Bear* was introduced as a play by a well-known author who wished to remain anonymous. Actually, it was by Josef Menzel, and was a rough paraphrase of a Russian fairy tale. It was not the publicity, but the play itself, with its simple appeal, which attracted crowds to the hall. *Basil and the Bear* was the most successful play ever put on at the Wooden Theatre, but unfortunately it was the only real success achieved there. It was followed by *Christmas at the Fireflies* by Trnka and his collaborator J. Kuncman, and another play by Josef Menzel, *Mr. Eustachius, the Dog and the Sultan*, which had the atmosphere of an Oriental fairy tale, and seems to have been something of an artistic achievement. But neither of these plays was as warmly received by the audience and the critics as *Basil and the Bear*.

Trnka was never able to put on any performances for adults. Throughout the autumn season the theatre just managed to keep its head above water, and the winter brought only a slight improvement. With the first days of spring, the audience fell off, and the theatre finished the season only with great difficulty. It was never to open again.

There were several reasons for Trnka's failure. Josef Skupa had not turned professional until the fame of the Holiday Camp Theatre had been firmly established, not only in Plzeň, but in the whole country and beyond. His name had, in fact, become a household word, and his puppets attracted theatre-goers everywhere. Trnka, in following Skupa's example, had failed to take this into account, and had turned professional before he and his company had acquired a name, or established any tradition of their own. Then, Trnka had also conceived his enterprise on too grand a scale to pay. Expenses were heavy: his staff of twenty-four all had to be paid.

There were other reasons, too. Trnka's interest in art dominated in his theatre, while producing was his weakest side. He did not study his audience sufficiently in his choice of play. The two plays about insects which he wrote in collaboration were copies of plays by Skupa, featuring *Dad Spejbl* and his son *Hurvínek*. But these were taken straight from life, and they made a definite point about children's education. They were appealing to children for this reason. Trnka and Kuncman produced only an imitation: a shell, and an empty one at that.

The two plays by Menzel were more

effective. *Basil and the Bear*, being based on a folk tale, was in key with a child's imagination, and had the sort of simple poetry that children understand. It was the story of the peasant Basil, and his fight with a bear. The clock, the chairs, the oven and the table, all came to life, and the cock, goat and pig, all took part. This was something a child could understand without much difficulty. *Mr. Eustachius, the Dog and the Sultan* was more complex, and, to judge by the reviews and the script, it gave scope for Trnka's leaning towards lyricism and his skill in stage design. It seems to have been the artistic highlight of the Wooden Theatre. But even so, it could not keep the theatre open after February.

TRNKA was deeply disappointed by the failure of his theatre, all the more because he had felt this to be the thing he did best, and he had planned to make it his future.

But, strangely enough, the failure of the puppet theatre coincided with his first major success as an illustrator. He was still earning a regular income from magazines, and his reputation had grown. Now he was invited to illustrate a book by Vítězslav Šmejc, *Mr. Boška's Tiger*.

Success as Children's Book Illustrator
Bruin the Bear *and others*
Style and Technique
The Children's Painter Exhibition

3

BECAUSE the puppet films through which Trnka became famous followed upon his work as an illustrator of children's books, attempts have been made to trace the characters in his films, and his development as an artist, back to his drawings. This, of course, is a mistake, and can only result in a superficial, distorted impression. Trnka was a puppeteer before he became an illustrator, and puppetry was his dominating passion. His drawings derived from his puppets, rather than the other way round. His drawings, of course, had their own influence in preparing him for his later work, but it was of a secondary nature.

The fact that his drawings derived from his puppets is plainly shown by his first successful illustrations. These were for a book by Josef Menzel, entitled *Bruin Furryball in his Forest Home*. This was an expanded version of Menzel's puppet play, *Bruin the Bear*, the big success of the Wooden Theatre. Trnka's illustrations were based upon the original wooden puppets who acted in the play. Puppets also inspired the illustrations to the books by Jan Karafiát, which were expanded versions of the puppet plays

Among the Fireflies and *Winter at the Fireflies*. When he illustrated *Caravan* by Wilhelm Hauff, he modelled his drawings on the puppets who had acted in Menzel's play, the Oriental fairy tale, *Mr. Eustachius, the Dog and the Sultan*.

Illustration, which Trnka regarded as a side-line, now had to take the place of his chief love, puppetry. His talent and personality were too strong for it to prove a blind alley. His art continued to develop, and he had a powerful influence upon Czech children's books, and the whole technique of illustration.

He may, in fact, be said to have revolutionised it. *Bruin Furryball in his Forest Home* was the sensation of the Christmas book trade in 1939. Trnka was still experimenting. He used contrasting patches of colour instead of outlined drawings, and the effect of the pure colours, without gradations in tone, was simple but original. Basil the peasant had a red nose, a brown moustache and a brown beard. Bruin had a white front, goggle eyes, and a red dot for a tongue. Trnka's characteristic of rounding off the form of his characters, combined with touches of the grotesque, made the pictures distinctive and exactly in key with the atmosphere of the text. He kept closely to the story, but suc-

ceeded also in conveying the spirit of it, as well as the events. Children responded at once to the poetry of his simple little drawings.

In his hands the illustrations became, not an extra, but an organic part of a children's book. This was a novel approach which helped to increase the artistic value of children's books : a book began to be something which, by its very appearance, could appeal to a child's imagination. Trnka regarded his illustrations as a starting-point of fantasy, rather than a means of directing the imagination. His pictures were intended to be the first link in a chain of associations. That is why he often did not depict any one action, or section of a story, but a whole array of events, in which dream bordered on reality, reality on fantasy.

Thus he gave a new meaning to the illustrator's work. The works of his early period varied in style and technique. He approached each book differently, as though he were testing the potentialities of the methods of reproduction. He used large loosely applied patches of colour, simple black and white lines, light water colours, and intricate techniques in which drawing and gouache were combined.

In the *Fireflies* books he used a technique

sharply contrasting with that of *Bruin the Bear*. The insects are drawn with thin lines, and he creates a world of tiny creatures dressed in period clothes, their behaviour in keeping with these. By tiny touches, such as the angle at which he sets the eyes, antennae and wings, he indicates the dream world, the world of insects.

Basil and the Bear, and a design for the illustrations for *Bruin the Bear*

The full-page illustrations are in bright coloured paint thinly applied. Trnka used a kind of spiral composition, building up his ideas from the top downwards. By linking certain shades of colour, and by the use of thin lines, he managed to convey the idea of weightlessness and irreality. The dream became real, and reality turned back into a dream.

This variety of techniques led only gradually to a unified style. Trnka was feeling his way towards it, and it took him some time to find it. But the basic concept never changed. Trnka did not illustrate scenes or situations. He mirrored the atmosphere, the dramatic or poetic meaning of the story.

The first book in which his individual approach as an illustrator took definite shape was *Susan Discovers the World*, by H. Chvojková. It was, in fact, a little book written by his wife about their daughter Susan's first steps into the bigger world, and it was a powerful source of inspiration to Trnka. It had double-page illustrations in which he developed his notion of reality combined with dream, in a way which was to become typical of all his work, not only as an illustrator. For the first time, he used a number of separate events to compose one illustration, placing them side by side for the sake of their association, at times superimposing or overlapping them, or linking them by an inner poetry, stressed outwardly through colour.

By painting the dreamlike aspects of reality Trnka was doing the same as the surrealists, but his illustrations have none of the cruelty or artistic ruthlessness of surrealism. His roaming brush reflected a child's roaming mind, with its inability to concentrate, its tendency to fantasy. He created a world where a lion leaps out of the sea on to the shore; where bears on ice floes admire floating roses; where the body of a drowned man sinks to the bottom through the seaweed; where a princess lights a stove, and a rider calms his prancing horse. The events seem unconnected, but everything is really subtly inter-related and full of magic, like an enchanting fairy-tale vision. Trnka had the gift of endowing animals and things with a mysterious and splendid inner life. His baby elephant suggests a toy for a small child; his water-lily a cradle. He draws a fish telling a fairy tale. His squirrel, hare and fawn are companions. Remote objects seem close, intimate, utterly gentle.

Even where he did not use puppets as models, his figures were reminiscent of them. He never attempted to conceal that he was at

Illustration for the book *The Fireflies*

heart a puppeteer. He drew attention to the relationship between his two mediums of expression in his first exhibition.

This was held at the Arts and Crafts Museum in Prague, between November 29th, 1940 and January 5th, 1941, under the title 'The Children's Painter'. Trnka laid his complete work before the public, putting his puppets side by side with his illustrations. He showed, not only the puppets from the Wooden Theatre, but also those private puppets which he had continued to make over the years, for no special purpose: the old decorative puppets of characters from Shakespeare, or inspired by the works of Maeterlink, Zeyer, or Mozart. And by their side were new ones, made in his spare time, as a relaxation from the tension of the work on book illustrations. Like the toys his mother had made, they were sometimes of rag. Trnka had an understanding of the quality of material, and he could use fabric to express character. He made rag figures of Indians, foresters, chimney sweeps, old men, musicians. They were all charming, in spite of their clumsiness. They were intended as children's toys, and were sewn by Trnka himself, though he had designed them with an eye to mass production. He had dreams of replacing the ordinary mass-produced dolls, which he thought inartistic and unsuited to children's psychological needs. He put his rag dolls on exhibition to attract the attention of the public and also the toy-makers.

'The Children's Painter' exhibition was the event of the season. Its great attraction was the diorama *The Insect Wedding*, which excited the small visitors, and even won praise from the art critics, who were generally niggardly, since they did not take puppets and children's book illustrating seriously. The response from public and critics established Trnka in his position in the forefront as an illustrator.

One thing disappointed him, however. The toy-makers did not show the interest he had anticipated. There were some voices raised in the Press, drawing their attention to Trnka's dolls, but nothing came of it.

Trnka's second more carefully planned attempt to bring his puppets to life had failed.

Stage-designer for Prague National Theatre
Development as a Painter
Landscapes, Portraits, Still-lifes
Further Book Illustration

4

TRNKA had hoped to turn the Wooden Theatre into a successful professional puppet theatre. He had failed, but the failure had been balanced by the great success of his illustrations for children's books. He had hoped that his rag puppets would revolutionise children's toys, but his ambitious plans had come to nothing. But again the failure was balanced by success, for the exhibition gained him fame and opened the door to the theatre. It seemed that it was always his side-line which brought him success, and that, in the field dearest to his heart, he was to experience failure after failure. Yet puppets continued to absorb him and to draw him to an extraordinary extent, even when he tried to turn to other things.

Now orders for illustrations were pouring in. He found them restricting, like a suit of heavy armour. He kept trying to escape, feeling frustrated, but then he would humbly return. In his moments of relaxation he would stoop over his puppets again, only to lay them aside once more. He was beginning to despair of ever finding a use for them.

During the period 1940 to 1945 he scattered his energies in a variety of directions.

His work during this time seems outwardly harmonious and well-balanced, but to look into it closely is to detect his feeling of nervousness and uncertainty. The work is varied, and at times the different pieces of work seem at variance with each other. By comparing them we can detect his pride and despair, his fits of hopelessness. He felt that he was not using his gifts to the full. He began to work for the theatre: the real theatre, not that of puppets, and he also sought an outlet for his creative urge in oil painting and graphic design.

While Trnka had been preparing his exhibition 'The Children's Painter', he had met Jiří Frejka, the producer of the National Theatre in Prague. He already knew a certain amount about stage design, from his work

A rag angel doll

with the puppet theatre. Nor was he a complete greenhorn at designing stage scenery for the large theatre. He had already done some casual work in this direction, producing simple designs distinguishable from his designs for puppet plays largely by the fact that the indications along the margins did not include such directions as 'neck $3^1/_2$ cm' 'arm 30 cm' 'leg 30 cm'. Back in Plzeň he had helped Josef Skupa to design the sets for the opera *Radúz and Mahulena* by Zeyer.

But Trnka's exhibition, especially the insect diorama, showed his potentialities as a stage designer. Also, he felt the need for work in another sphere, as a release from book illustration. An invitation to work for the National Theatre came just at the right moment.

FEBRUARY 1940 saw the opening night of Goldoni's *Venetian Carnival*, with stage designs by J. Trnka. This was the beginning of several years' work for the National Theatre.

Trnka's technique as a stage designer was also only at its beginning. But its basis was the same as that of his illustrations, and typical of him. He did not seek external motifs, so much as inner themes, concerning himself with the atmosphere of the play, its moods and emotions. He placed the emphasis on colour and visual effect. He tried to create an active setting for the play, instead of a static picture. His design for *The Venetian Carnival* was conceived in the form of a semicircular horizon. Certain sections turned and opened for the different scenes, producing an impression of a constantly changing environment. This horizon was simply drawn, and the actors stood outlined against it. The whole thing was faintly reminiscent of a book illustration in *Susan Discovers the World*. He united apparently disconnected scenes and themes, so that they made an impact as a whole. He regarded the stage as something more than an effective setting for the actors: to him, it was an integral part of the play, of the 'willing suspension of disbelief'. Its function was to produce enchantment: a dream.

It was typical of Trnka's sense of unity that he was not content merely to design the stage set, but also designed the costumes, and in his later plays went even further and involved himself in the production.

The Venetian Carnival was followed by Shakespeare's *A Winter's Tale*. Again he used a simple, colourful design. The play

Stage designs for *The Strakonice Bagpiper:* The Forester's Hut

was being produced at the time of the German Occupation, and the references in it to a powerful kingdom of Bohemia sounded a patriotic note. Trnka's designs showed his awareness of the new meaning the play had acquired. He designed the Sicilian scenes in black and white, and those set in Bohemia in colour. He used tapestries in the Sicilian scenes to produce a sense of the past, while in the Bohemian scenes he conveyed the

In Turkey

intimate charm of nature, the lyrical landscapes of his native country.

His meaning came through clearly to both
audience and critics, who appreciated the
note of optimism. It was perhaps the favourable reaction to *A Winter's Tale* that gave
Frejka and Trnka the idea of producing a
series of Czech classics at the National Theatre.
Their work together reached its peak
with these plays. The original intention was

Under the Gallows

to produce a series of four, but, owing to the Occupation, they were able to produce only two. There was nearly a year between the first nights of these two plays, but they show a common inspiration, and they represent Trnka's finest work as a stage designer. Each is in his lyrical mood; each is a painter's dream. He never surpassed them in any later designs.

Trnka's work with the National Theatre

came to an end in 1944. He had not finished with stage design, however, and later he entered for a competition to design the stage sets for Smetana's opera *Libuše*. He won the first prize, but the Germans forbade the opera to be performed. They suppressed anything which they thought might lead to an upsurge of national feeling, or to a belief that the Germans could be defeated.

This opera, however, brought Trnka his first encounter with the old legends of Bohemia, and it revealed his strong feeling for ancient traditional themes. This was something he was to develop many years later in his film *Old Czech Legends*.

Trnka's work for the theatre represents an important phase in his development. But it was only one of several activities he was engaged in at the time.

TRNKA'S URGE to paint had found stimulus in both book illustrations and stage design. But he found both these mediums inhibiting, since his imagination was restricted by the text. He wanted a freer means of self-expression, and so he turned to pure painting. His paintings are deeply revealing of his psychological make-up, probably because he did not really feel at home as a painter, and thus involuntarily betrayed himself. In art, as in life, it is the weak moments which are the most revealing. But of all the things we learn about Trnka from his painting, the chief is that, whatever else he did, he always remained a puppeteer at heart.

At the time when Trnka came to Prague, artists were seeking for new forms to build up the ruins of shape, which had been broken down by Cubism. Trnka was not interested in problems of that kind, nor in artistic conflicts. The worlds of Picasso, Braque, Léger or Matisse did not concern him. He always remained indifferent to any experiments with pure form. An introspective artist, he was interested in form solely as a means of expressing his own vision. It was, of course, a dream: a puppeteer's vision. His world never extended beyond the little figurines and dolls, toys with their own landscapes, their own

A design for Smetana's opera *Libuše*

houses. He left it to other painters to attempt to express reality by an attack upon the subconscious mind with bizarre shapes. In his paintings he created a reality of his own: his own special world apart. It was a world full of fantastic dreams and lyrical delight: a world of dolls, removed from the theatre and bewitched into stillness on the canvas. It is this which gives his paintings their remoteness.

There was, of course, a paradox in the situation. Trnka had turned to painting in order to express himself, and to escape from the limitations imposed by illustration and stage design, which bound the artist to a literary theme. Yet, when he tried to interpret his own vision, he found that he could not escape the literary inspirations of folk culture, of the theatre, of classical literature. He was conscious of this paradox, and found it hard to accept the fact that his attempt to break away had only led him back to his starting-point. He tried to avoid 'puppet' themes, and turned to landscape painting and portraiture, flowers and still-life. But a change of subject was not the answer: he could not escape from himself. His lack of involvement in artistic movements, a certain slackness, even, in his approach to the technical problems of painting, were probably because the paintings were a subconscious substitute for a medium he had not yet found. He was preparing for something that was yet to come.

It is interesting, however, to examine his paintings, not for their importance as works of art, but for what they reveal about Trnka himself.

His painting had, of course, a movement and logic of its own. This is shown most clearly in those which are inspired by the theatre. In some of his earlier paintings, such as 'Comedians', 'The Poor Man's Circus', 'Masquerades', he is doing little more than express the nostalgic or exotic atmosphere of the setting. In such later paintings as 'Mime', 'Actors', 'Clowns', the made up face begins to reveal a second, deeper, more real face: the face of the man. Like Degas, he attempted to capture in paint the man behind the mask or costume. The resemblance was purely one of theme and setting: Trnka's paintings had none of the harmony to be found in Degas. The travelling comedians of Trnka's theatre and circus seem to have put on their costumes in an attempt to escape from ordinary life into the world of fantasy and make-believe. He shows the theatre as something apart from life. Often the comedians' effort to escape seems desperate, and the theatre is an attempt to ridicule life. The grinning mask and buffoonery hide fear of the moment when the comedy is over. These paintings can be most fully understood when they are seen in

Theatre (oil painting)

Poor Man's Circus (oil painting)

Theatrical Motif
(oil painting)

their relationship to the atmosphere of the war years.

By contrast, Trnka's landscapes, especially 'Spring', 'Autumn' and 'Winter', were among the purest in feeling of the paintings: the dream of beauty had returned. He did not paint an actual landscape, nor depict nature in any definite aspect. Instead, he created through his imagination the type of a Czech winter, autumn and spring, conveying an impression of each season through the predominance of certain colours and objects. Winter is seen in bright tones. In this painting and in 'Autumn' there are scenes which recall those of Trnka's childhood.

'Spring', 'Autumn', and 'Winter' became, with 'Bethlehem', the most popular and best known of all Trnka's paintings. 'Bethlehem' is one of Trnka's largest canvases, and the most complex in composition. It comes closer than any other painting to interpreting his vision of men in terms of puppets and toys. The design and landscape are faintly reminiscent of a Breughel painting. The foreground was painted in thick paint, in a warm basic tone, white to yellow with brown predominating. The more distant landscape was painted in thinner paint, and is expressive of Trnka's lyricism. The crib and the Madonna are in the centre, surrounded by the worshipping Kings and a group of carol singers. From the left a gamekeeper with a hare is hurrying to the scene followed by an old man, his ears protected against the frost. Three musicians are hesitantly approaching the crib from the right. In the background are the typical contours of a snow-clad Czech landscape. A waggon is seen driving to the mill; gallows stand on the hill top; in the distance is the onion tower of a church.

In these paintings Trnka was able to paint his own vision: his own inner world of poetic dreams. In the still-lifes, the flower paintings, and especially the portraits, he had to depict given reality. He achieved a varying degree of success. He tried to infuse poetry into his flowers and still-lifes, but they seem almost conventional, and he did not manage to overcome his tendency to descriptiveness. Themes that presented painters with problems of form remained alien to him, and he dealt with them only in order to experiment in different genres.

Autumn (oil painting)

Bethlehem (oil painting)

In portraiture he found subjects closer to his heart, for problems in psychology were involved. Trnka's portraits are impressive: in spite of a somewhat traditional style of painting, they reveal the dominant characteristics of the sitters.

The finest is his magnificent portrait of his mother. It is more than a portrait: it is a study in biography, a son's expression of love and respect. The old woman's head is gently bowed, her hair is untidy, her tired eyes and her nose are expressive of content. Trnka shows the inner pride of a simple but unusual woman: determination, clarity, certainty are all apparent in her glance. Trnka and his mother had certain features and certain psychological traits in common, and the look upon her face was to be shown later upon his own in several self-portraits which he painted.

Trnka's self-portraits were made between 1939 and 1945. The first two are not particularly interesting. The earliest depicts a fairly attractive young man with a moustache and a scar across his face. In the second his strength is emphasised, and the scar is shown as a symbol of pride. The others are more revealing. In the self-portrait painted in 1943 Trnka adopts a stylised technique, showing himself in a simple yellow shirt, against a grey background. The head is strong and proudly raised; the scar is again stressed. The technique is simpler than in the other two, and more unified. Where they showed a young man, this depicts a man of strong, more mature personality. Even during this period of search and experiment, discontent and scattered activity, Trnka was aware of his own powers as an artist, and confident that he had a future. He did not know in what direction it lay, but he felt certain of great achievement, and he inscribed this certainty on his own face. His last self-portrait is not quite so balanced, but it shows a similar confidence. It is a deeper, more expressive portrait.

Winter (oil painting)

Zuzanka (oil painting)

Self-Portrait, 1944
(oil painting)

Bagpiper (oil painting)

Illustration for the book *Caravan*

DURING this period, illustration had taken third place in Trnka's activities. This is shown by the diminishing number of published books. In 1940 nine books with his illustrations were published. In 1941 there were only six. In 1942 there were five. In the last two years of the war he published only one book each year. The illustrations themselves showed progress, however, and were considerably influenced by his work in stage design and pure painting.

Again there was a paradox. In pure painting, Trnka had difficulty in expressing himself freely, since he could not escape from literary themes. In illustration he began to achieve a greater purity than before, and a

classical maturity. This was first apparent in his illustrations to *Susan Discovers the World*. But it becomes more marked as the influence of his free work in oils begins to appear on his illustrations.

During this time he illustrated several books in which he gave full reign to his imagination, expressing the poetry and mystery to which children respond in reading. This is particularly true of his illustrations

for *Caravan* by Wilhelm Hauff, and *Say It with Me*, a book of children's verses by František Hrubín.

These two books represent the two extremes of Trnka's work as an illustrator. Hauff's fairy stories were intended for older children. Trnka took his inspiration from the East, creating an exotic world of sultans, sheikhs, camels, jinns. Again he concentrated upon conveying the atmosphere of the story, rather than depicting any one situation. An illustration, while closely related to a given story, would evoke dream images outside its actual events, though arising from them. Each story had a black and white chapter heading, which was part of the ornamentation of the initial beginning of the chapter, and the whole book had ten full page coloured illustrations. Trnka used a technique of Indian ink and water colour which he had borrowed from the painters of the Far East. His drawing was extremely fine, with bright paint. The large size of the book gave him a chance to express himself without fear of the fineness of his drawing being spoilt by reproduction. It is difficult to find words for the impressive effect which he achieved by means of unusual composition, the use of colour, and the technique of drawing with a hair-thin brush.

Hrubín's book of children's rhymes, *Say It with Me*, was meant for children of pre-school age and younger schoolchildren. Here Trnka became an equal partner of the poet,

Illustrations for the book *Czech Fairy Tales* by Jiří Horák

and though the first edition bore only the poet's name, all subsequent editions had Trnka's name as well, an outer confirmation of the place of the illustrations as an integral part of the book, the drawings complementing the poems, and vice versa. Trnka made a coloured lithograph for each of Hrubín's verses. The intimate world of tiny creatures created by Hrubín gave infinite scope to Trnka's art, and his puppeteer's vision is strikingly exemplified. It was particularly well suited to the vision of a child, where proportions change, and conventions are broken down. Trnka's drawings were simple, the colours unexpected. Sturdy little boys, chubby-faced little girls, miniature birds and fishes, all look as though they have escaped from a puppet theatre. Two little hands are needed to hold a pencil, and a little cooking-pot is as large as one of the figures. They all look as though they have settled down for a moment on the page, but are ready to run away and turn somersaults to amuse the small readers.

Illustrations for the book *Grimm's Fairy Tales*

TWO DAYS before the end of the Second World War Trnka had his thirtieth birthday. What had he so far achieved? He was a well-known illustrator and stage designer. The days were over when he had had to receive his midday meal from the Bohemian Heart. He was successful, and books which he had illustrated were selling well. His opinion was sought and valued on the subject of book illustration. He had also put his abilities as a painter to the test, and had studied the work of other artists: the art of China and Japan; Czech Gothic painting and the artists of the National Revival; Breughel, Rembrandt, Watteau and Corot; the early Italian Renaissance, and the lyricism of Botticelli.

Trnka knew, however, that all this was only a preparation for greater achievement. He felt that he had latent strength as an artist, which was still waiting for the impulse and opportunity to break through and show itself. He had not forgotten the puppets.

An epoch in Trnka's life was ending, just as an epoch in history was also coming to a close. The thunder of the Red Army guns that could be heard in the distance during the quiet of the night foretold a new era.

Trnka had no clear idea of the next step but he felt that there would be new opportunities for his creative urge. His grand dream returned: the dream that had been shattered by hard facts when he opened the Wooden Theatre.

Times were different now, and nine years of work had made Trnka a different man.

On a theme by Rembrandt (drawing)

5

MAY 5th, 1945, was the day of the Prague Uprising, and four days later came Liberation Day. Trnka felt the upsurge of national excitement: a desire to rebuild and re-create was in the air. He had always worked hard, and now he felt his energies redoubled. He began to look for a medium which really suited him, and it was then that he had the idea of experimenting with the puppet film. He thought of a theme, and began to write the script of a puppet tale called *Grandpa Planted a Beet*.

It was inevitable, however, that Trnka should be side-tracked from his puppets once again. His desire to experiment with films happened to coincide with the formation of a group of artists and animators who were initiating a revival in animated cartoons. They invited Trnka to take charge of the work. Since he did not feel fully prepared for work with his puppets, he agreed.

Trick Brothers, as the group called themselves, had arisen out of the Trick Studios, where they drew captions and made trick sets for films. At the outbreak of war, this had become a refuge for numerous young artists and architects. They had been under the

From the cartoon film *Grandpa Planted a Beet*

management of Diellens, an Austrian, whose ideas for animated cartoons had included a cartoon based on the opera *Orpheus and Eurydice*, for which life drawings were made of several well-known singers. Diellens had left at the beginning of 1943, and the studio had come under the supervision of von Möllendorf, a Nazi, who had taken very little interest in the work. They had completed a cartoon called *Wedding in the Coral Sea*, which was technically brilliant, but character-less. The story was typical of the time of the German occupation, and the characterisation showed the influence of Walt Disney.

Walt Disney had, in fact, dominated animated cartoons throughout the thirties. It was not only that the market was flooded with films from his own studios, but also that he had influenced the technique and style all over the world. A cartoon film was automatically thought of as a Disney film, and any work in Europe in this field was always along his lines. Disney's stock-in-trade was in general use. He nearly always used anthropomorphism, creating a number of standard animal figures, whom he made resemble human beings. To some extent, Donald Duck, Mickey Mouse, Pluto and the rest acted out the minor worries of the average middle-class American. The basic ideas were the same as those which had been expressed in the silent film, but the use of animal characters made them funnier and more original. There was usually the same moral: the characters had to keep smiling whatever complicated events overtook them, and the comic side of the ordinary man's daily life was emphasised. Disney was assured of a steady market. His monopoly lasted fifteen years, and no innovator was ever able to break into the field during that time.

Then came Trnka and the Trick Brothers. Years later, Stephen Bosustow, the American critic, was to call Trnka 'the first rebel against Disney's omnipotence'.

Disney's omnipotence had helped other

Grandpa Planted a Beet (outline)

animators to learn the basic elements of the craft. His cartoons had given them technique and skill. But what they lacked was a style and concept of their own. These Trnka was to supply in his very first film, made immediately after the war.

Trnka came to the company with the script which he had originally planned as a puppet film: *Grandpa Planted a Beet*. He adapted it instead as an animated cartoon, designing the figures himself. The studio, which had not yet officially taken the name Trick Brothers,

From the cartoon film *The Animals and the Brigands*

started work as a subsidiary of the newly established Film Institute, on June 15th, a month and six days after the end of the war. The film *Grandpa Planted a Beet* was a turning-point both for Jiří Trnka and for the Czech cinema. Czechoslovakia had taken a revolutionary step in the field of the animated cartoon. *Grandpa Planted a Beet* was the harbinger of a new era, and was warmly welcomed in its own country, as the first truly Czech animated cartoon.

The moral of *Grandpa Planted a Beet* was simple but not obvious: that the help of even the smallest and weakest is valuable. There was no Disney-like anthropomorphism. Man remained man, and the animals remained animals. The two worlds were not interchangeable.

Technically, the film reflected Trnka's experiences in the puppet theatre and as an illustrator. He could not throw off these two influences, knowing nothing about films and having therefore nothing to substitute for them. This was a weakness to some extent, but also a strength. It prevented him from copying. He brought a fresh vision to the cinema, and thus, ignorant though he was of film-making, he produced a work of importance.

The setting of *Grandpa Planted a Beet* was confined entirely to the inside of the cottage and the cottage garden. It was faintly reminiscent of a puppet set. And there was a night scene which recalled some of the ideas in *Basil and the Bear*, the one success of the Wooden Theatre. The animation was rather clumsy. The film was a little like a book illustration in motion. But compared with the American cartoons it was a real discovery. The artistic level was high, and new ground had been broken.

Grandpa Planted a Beet was followed by a whole series of cartoons made under Trnka in the Trick Brothers Studio: *The Animals and the Brigands* (from the story 'The Enchanted Wood'), *The Gift*, a parody, and *The Chimney Sweep*, an anti-Nazi satire. *Grandpa Planted a Beet* had achieved a warm welcome in Czechoslovakia. *The Animals and the Brigands* broke through internationally: it was acclaimed at the first International Film Festival at Cannes.

The Animals and the Brigands was based on a well-known fairy tale about the animals in the forest who frighten the brigands and take their money. In Trnka's version the brigands became three harmless creatures. The animals, too, were frightened by the mysteries of the forest at night. Trnka made the forest into a kind of poetical and fantastic dream, in which mushrooms and acorns came to life, the light of dawn dispelling the terrifying aspect of the noctural moth. The setting and technique were forerunners of those Trnka was to use more freely in depicting the forest creatures, the Athenian lovers, and the artisans in *A Midsummer Night's Dream*. His approach was a continuation of the methods he had used in *Grandpa Planted a Beet*, but the cartoon was more professional in character and better as a film. The drawing and animation were greatly improved, and the story gave scope for a larger set, more development, and speedier action. He sometimes made deliberate use of delayed climax, by lingering over lyrical detail, and this was to become characteristic of his work in the puppet film. There was one episode in *The Animals and the Brigands*, an encounter between the animals and brigands in a cottage and the panic-stricken flight of each group in a different direction, which showed that he was now handling animation and composition with mastery. It was a technical triumph for this new type of animated cartoon. A moving camera was used. There were close-ups for added drama, and panoramic effects for breadth.

The Animals and the Brigands was typically Czech. When the film was first performed, people began to speak of a Czech school of cartoon films. The reviews in Czechoslovakia and elsewhere, when the film was performed at Cannes, confirmed that Trnka and the Trick Brothers had embarked on a promising road, and that there had at last been a breakaway from the school of Walt Disney.

Despite the success of these two films, Trnka remained dissatisfied. He felt that he was still on the threshold of what could be achieved, and that he needed to produce something more ambitious to establish the new Czech school of rebels against Disney. He succeeded with his film *The Gift*.

The Gift revealed Trnka for the first time as a capable film director. It was full of excitement and ideas. Superficially, its aim was to parody the excessive zeal of film producers and authors, but its meaning really went further than that. Its apparent slightness did not conceal the serious purpose of satirising the ideals of bourgeois society. The cartoons were set inside an acted film. The drawing was simpler and more dynamic than in the preceding films. There were little figures drawn from popular Kitsch of that time, representing certain stock types: the Millionaire, the Artist, the Servant, 'such a faithful devoted soul'. The treatment was grotesque, and there was a spoken commentary which provided scope

From the cartoon film *The Gift*

for original associations of ideas in the
drawing. The story was full of surprises,
and there were rapid changes of setting: at
one moment the characters were in a large,
busy city, at another in the romantic sur-

roundings of Venice. *The Gift* had its own
poetry: it was aggressive, original, rich in
satire.

It was, however, ahead of its time, and
when it was first shown it was misunder-

stood. The critics found it incomprehensible, and accused Trnka of being deliberately odd and pretentious. They felt the film was a mistake, and detracted from his former successes. Today, however, the meaning which baffled the critics in 1946 is clear enough, for in the intervening years the animated cartoon has become established, and its idiom is more easily understood. To-day, too, the influence of *The Gift* on ani-

because it satisfied the need to laugh at the recent past, and thus relieve the protracted tension of the Occupation period. But, though it was about recent events, it remains alive and topical, carrying a warning of some urgency.

mated films in general can be more fully appreciated. This influence exerted itself gradually, both at home and abroad.

Stephen Bosustow, who had been Disney's disciple, but rebelled against his master's influence, owed much to Trnka's *The Gift* when, some years later, he began to make his own ironic cartoons ridiculing the American bourgeoisie. Vukotic, the Jugoslav film-producer, also owes much to the influence of *The Gift*.

The Chimney Sweep, Trnka's next film, was a political satire. Trnka used two simple main characters, Springer, a chimney-sweep, and a snooping collaborator. He caricatured the goose-stepping S.S. men, and the film was full of comedy, action, and dramatic chases, but the satire also was strong. Trnka made use of what he had learned in producing *The Gift*, but *The Chimney Sweep*, was more direct and simpler. It was understood readily, and the critics regarded it as one of Trnka's best films.

It was received so favourably at that time

WITH *The Chimney Sweep*, Trnka's work in cartoon films came to an end. He designed the scenery for the fable of *The Fox and the Jug*, and then he moved into a small studio in the upper storey of an old house in the centre of Prague, where he finally turned to puppet films. Some of the animators from the cartoon films joined him here, and he also found a kindred spirit to help him in Václav Trojan, the composer.

Trnka was now turning back to his puppets, fully prepared for the first time, since he now had had much varied experience, in art, puppetry, animated cartoons, and life in general. The circumstances were very different from those which had previously led to failure. He could rely on the solid backing of the nationalised film industry.

Trnka abandoned animated cartoons as he had abandoned book illustration, without

regrets. Though he was leaving a well-established art form he had helped to develop, he felt strong and confident in venturing on to new ground. He set out into uncharted territory, and he found himself.

The collaborator in the cartoon film *The Chimney Sweep*

6

BY THE AUTUMN of 1946, when he first entered the little studio of his own to breathe life into his puppets, Trnka was thirty-four, mature as a man and an artist. Up till that time, his life had been one long apprenticeship. Now he had come to the turning-point in his development, and he was to continue to dedicate himself to his chosen art.

His face and appearance at this time reveal his maturity. Photographs taken from 1947 onwards show him almost the same as he was in 1960. His fairish hair, combed back, falls loosely over his ears, and hangs down upon his rather thick neck. An impression of generosity is added by his big straw-coloured moustache. His slanting, heavy-lidded eyes look at the world with a certain lively scrutiny. The deepening wrinkles, the increased fleshiness of face and figure, and the marked scar across his right cheek are the only evidence to be found in the later photographs of the passing of the years. Trnka has been said to resemble various famous historical characters, among them Balzac. Such resemblances are generally superficial and accidental, but Trnka and Balzac had in common a certain monumental quality in their appearance. With Trnka, there is something paradoxical and incongruous in the fact that, sturdy as he was, he should all his life have been drawn to the delicate world of the puppet. His work is fine and fragile. His fleshy, thick fingers are highly sensitive. In this, Trnka is the true descendant of the Czech peasant and craftsman: under his touch, wood, cloth, glass and metal turn into living things.

The puppets were set out on one table in a manger scene, with a camera and a couple of spotlights. He was about to begin work on a film called *Bethlehem*, which was to have been an experimental film, made largely to test the potentialities of the new techniques. He had no idea that it would lead to a complete cycle of films, called *The Czech Year*, and that it was in fact the basic chord out of which he was to build the six movements of a suite. It embodied all the themes of his future work, later to be developed independently and with more profundity. For the first time Trnka was expressing his true inner self, the breath of his being. *Bethlehem* contained his whole philosophy, which he expressed later in different ways, but never actually altered. He had now passed the borderline from a proficient artist to a great one.

Trnka was and remained a humanist, linked by a myriad fine threads to the traditions of the country which had bred him. Though he might seem at times to have been submerged in his puppeteer's dream of beauty, he was keenly aware of the problems in the world round him, and he also had an almost seismographic sense of impending upheavals. This often made him ahead of his time, and consequently his work was better understood after a lapse of time. He decisively condemned war, ridiculing the beating of the war drums, the stupidity of military drill and the subordination of the individual, and he showed his concern at any threat to world peace. On the other hand, he exalted the greatness of those who would defend with the sword their right to life and liberty in their homeland. He extolled the wisdom of the common man, and the sweetness of a man content at his work. He deplored the cleavage that exists between civilisation and true culture, intellect and spirit, technique and art. He condemned artificiality and voiced his own love of unspoilt nature and open spaces.

Bethlehem was to be the last part of the cycle *The Czech Year*, but it was the first to be made, and was completed independently of the others, which developed out of it. It illustrates the organic development of Trnka's work, for it had grown out of his illustrations and paintings, just as the illustrations and paintings had grown out of his work in the puppet theatre.

The ideas he had expressed in his films were the same as those in his book illustrations and paintings, but he was now no longer limited by the static medium, which had allowed him to do no more than stimulate the imagination. His figures had seemed as though, despite an urge to move about and play out their parts, they had been transfixed in one pose and one place. Previously he had tried to overcome this limitation by combining different themes in one picture, in order to express a deeper meaning. Now, armed with the magically-endowed film camera, spot-lights and three-dimensional puppets, instead of flat drawings, he could speak out more fully. *Bethlehem*, like his first animated cartoon, produces the impression of an animated illustration. Because it was made first, before he was fully experienced, it is the weakest in story and animation of the six parts of *The Czech Year*. But it has, all the same, his characteristic poetic vision, and feeling for his native land. There is hardly any story. The film begins with shots of the traditional Christmas carp, nuts and apples on a plate, a Christmas loaf. The sound of carols rouses the shepherds, the neighbours, the musicians, the game-keeper, and the carols continue as background music while these groups all move through the snowy landscape towards the manger. *Bethlehem* is no more than the picture Trnka had painted many years previously brought to life, except that the puppet film version was more crowded with figures, and had greater breadth. But all the individual figures had been taken over, as well as the composition of the final scene.

It was, as we have seen, the chord out of which he built the six movements of the film *The Czech Year*, in which he depicted the year in the Czech countryside. Each part was more or less independent: the mood was lyrical or epic, and the story was accompanied and often borne along by music and folk songs. The first part was *Carnival*, with bagpipes playing for the parade of masked figures on the snow-covered village green in front of the cottages. There are revels, and groups of rustic mummers, including a performing bear with his master. At the moment of climax, the music leads on to the next part.

This is *Spring*, symbolised by children's games. Their voices are heard singing songs

From *The Czech Year*

Carnival

Spring

and rhymes. The opening theme is departing winter, and the tune is nostalgic, but this is quickly replaced by the rhythm of dancers, and of a hunting tune. There is no attempt to tell a consecutive story by means either of the pictures or the songs, but there is a subtle relationship between the two, as song follows song, and sometimes the movements of the

children form a parallel to the images created by the songs, as, for instance, in the brisk children's dance which accompanies the song of the owl and the sparrow. At the end of *Spring* comes rest. After the busy day comes the evening; there is the music of a cradle song, and the moon rises in a clear sky.

Summer is depicted in two sequences, again linked by music. The opening scenes are of ripening cornfields and harvesters struggling against the thunder and rain. These are the setting for *The Legend of St. Procopius*. The legend of this peasant saint is told by an old man, sitting with a candle alight beside him to drive away the thunderstorm.

Procopius was tilling the fields when a little devil came to tempt him by putting obstacles in the way of his work. He filled up the ploughed furrow with stone, and offered to make Procopius ruler of the world if he would abandon his work. In the end Procopius defeated the devil by patience and hard work, and the tempter himself pulled the plough, in order to experience work for himself.

In another legend, Procopius triumphed over a nobleman, and prevented him from killing the doe he had been hunting.

For the sequences dealing with the Slavonic saint, Trnka departed from the lyrical style of the earlier sequences, and adopted an epic manner. One can detect the influence of Gothic painting. The legends are nearer than any other part of *The Czech Year* to Trnka's later film, *Old Czech Legends*, but, despite the difference in style, they are still an integral part of the whole. In Trnka's hands the old legend of St. Procopius lost some of its miraculous content, and became a simple tale extolling peaceful human labour, which is shown triumphing over evil and the temptation to idleness.

The second part of the Summer sequence was *Pilgrimage* still linked to the sequences about St. Procopius, since it is towards a little chapel consecrated to him that the peasant pilgrims are shown winding their way through the fields. His victory over evil is still remembered, and is still part of the pattern. The procession is led by a choir leader and the village band. A little girl prays to be given a doll from the town; the lovers pray for their love to be returned; a little man prays for his one throw to topple all the ninepins.

Next came *Harvest Festival*. The village green is crowded with stalls and entertainments, and with excited villagers goggling at them. There are stalls selling marzipan hearts, magicians, cloth merchants, soothsayers, and strolling actors setting up their tent.

The climax to the excitement comes in a brilliantly conceived sequence in a puppet theatre. Here the leading puppet actor comes on the stage and, in the style of the old ballad singers, introduces a heart-breaking tale, which is acted to the accompaniment of songs:

'Once upon a time there was a squire. And he had a most beautiful daughter. Oh, master, master mine, and her name was Catherine . . .'

The naive audience, appreciative of melodrama, enjoy the tragic tale of the Turk and the Squire's Daughter. At its climax, it is dramatically interrupted by one of the audience who hurls himself on to the stage to prevent the puppet hangman from performing his evil act.

This sequence shows Trnka's complete mastery of his art: it is not only the best passage in *The Czech Year*, but is one of the best he ever achieved. He drew on his childhood experiences of folk puppetry, and its effect upon the audience. The simple people were enchanted by the skill of the puppeteers (who were Trnka's acknowledged predecessors), and regarded a play as real, to be experienced as such. Trnka took great trouble to distinguish between the people at the fair and the actors, who were meant to be puppets in a puppet comedy. Actually, of course, they were all puppets, but he made the real people distinct from the 'puppet' actors. The result was remarkably effective, and shows how deeply he entered into his subject.

There follows a short epilogue, where a gipsy plays a sorrowful tune on the fiddle as he bids farewell to the fair and to summer. This is followed by Autumn.

This sequence is the *Village Feast*. There is abundant food and drink, buns, pork, haggis and wine. The band is playing. From early morning all the peasants have been a little tipsy. And then, amid the feasting, music, and gaiety, there sounds, for a moment, a tragic note. Stout peasant women are seen offering dishes of buns to beggars standing supplicating with outstretched hands. A blind harp-player is singing a song about an evil soldier who destroys human happiness. In front of a crowded tavern an old man with one leg is performing a mournful dance. But the sequence ends on a humorous note. There is a fight at the inn, and the musicians are thrown out just as they are starting up the song: 'We met in joyous mood, and jovially we'll part'. They scatter to all sides, wishing everyone goodnight.

And then comes Winter, the scene of the Adoration, the sound of the carols, and the pilgrims arriving at Bethlehem: the sequence, in fact, which Trnka devised first, and which gave him the inspiration for the whole.

As we have seen, *The Czech Year* was not originally conceived as a definite cycle, and for that reason the individual parts are uneven in technique. *Bethlehem* was the weakest in story and animation. *Spring* is probably the most successful in animation, but its lyricism causes it to lack strength. The story and the general expression are at their purest in the Summer section: *The Pilgrimage* and *The Legend of Saint Procopius*. *The Feast*, though lacking in order and clumsy in animation, gives the impression of being a self-contained work, even the odd, accidentally included touches adding to its highly dramatic atmosphere.

In *The Czech Year* Trnka introduced some daring innovations. *Bethlehem* was descriptive, an illustration in motion, but in *The Feast* and in other parts of the cycle, he made use of highly original methods of expression through the medium of the films. By this time he had mastered the details of settings, camera positions and so on. But he had also discovered a form of expression of his own, full of evocative touches, symbols and images, which, together with Trojan's remarkable musical accompaniment, created a kind of poetry, which was, however, true to the film medium. Admittedly, some of Trnka's imagery is not easy to understand. Trojan sometimes had to suggest in his music what Trnka did not fully express. But this negative aspect of Trnka's work is not always a weakness. Sometimes it is an advantage, for it forces the spectator to participate, and thus to discover new and unexpected beauty.

IN THE SIXTY YEARS of Czechoslovakian film-making, there has hardly ever been a film accepted by the critics with such unreserved praise as that which they bestowed on *The Czech Year*. It was first shown shortly before Christmas in 1947, and within a few days praise was pouring in from all sides. The critics, in unusual unanimity, understood it. This reception confirmed for Trnka what he had known from the moment he began work on *Bethlehem*: this time the puppets would not disappoint him. Some people might have been excited by the acclamation. But Trnka remained more or less indifferent, as he later remained indifferent to attacks and criticism.

In fact, by the time it was being performed for the first time, *The Czech Year* already belonged to his past. He had by then started living in a new dream and doing new work. He had started to write the script for *The Emperor's Nightingale*.

From The Legend of St. Procopius

98

Pilgrimage

Harvest Festival

The Legend of St. Procopius

Bethlehem

Harvest Festival

7

FROM THE OPEN window of an old house set in a garden comes the sound of a piano. A boy is doing his exercises, trying hard to keep to the rhythm of the metronome. The room is dark, but outside the sun shines brightly. The boy is surrounded by a multitude of mechanical toys and . . . loneliness.

This is the opening scene of Trnka's version of Hans Andersen's famous tale *The Emperor's Nightingale*.

It has been said that the 'magic lamp of the Czech artist gave the jewel of the Danish poet a new lustre.'

In turning the story into a puppet film, Trnka used it as no more than raw material. It set a whole series of related motifs sounding in him. In *The Czech Year* the theme of the peasants' year had evoked a whole chain of folk images. In *The Emperor's Nightingale* the images were those evoked by the story itself, ranging through a whole scale of thoughts and feelings. His version was much wider in scope than Andersen's, but it retained its essential core. He took its pattern and spirit and transformed them for a new medium.

The subject attracted Trnka as much for its basic meaning as for the scope it gave for poetic expression in a puppet film. Andersen's nightingale was a symbol of the life-giving sun, and of the simple natural life triumphing over the conventions and mechanical aspect of staid society life. To stress this central idea, and to draw attention to the fact, the story grew out of real life, and was concerned with it, Trnka set his version within an acted frame. This was the story of a spoilt little boy from a rich family, closed in behind the walls of a Victorian mansion, and restricted by the care of his aunts. A little poor girl, cut off from the boy's life by a fence, embodies the natural, healthy life. The boy feels attracted to the girl's carefree games, but a new toy, a mechanical bird, makes him turn back again into the shadow of the house with its set customs. He falls ill, the doctor arrives, and in the night, in his fever, he begins to dream.

A book of Hans Andersen's Fairy Tales drops to the floor, and the main theme begins. Immediately the objects in the room undergo a strange transformation. A carved pipe takes on the face of a Chinese fisherman listening to the song of the nightingale. A traycloth becomes a fragile porcelain gate to the Imperial palace.

Trnka contrived to make the story about the Emperor a continuation of the story in the acted frame, about the little boy, by linking the two together through identical objects that appear in the little boy's surroundings and in the Chinese Emperor's palace, where they are key symbols. Thus one of the boy's aunts becomes a wrinkled faced courtier who forces the little boy to submit to the court ceremonial. The little girl recurs as the nightingale's friend, who lives outside the Emperor's palace; the doctor symbolises Death.

In Hans Andersen's tale the court is run on stupid, grotesque lines. Trnka carries it further and makes his court inhuman. The impression is all the more terrible because he conceives the Emperor as a child, a boy whose natural liking for play comes into conflict with the staid ceremonial forced on him by the courtiers. He is hopelessly isolated and lost among their serious, characterless faces and ceremonious movements.

The contrast between the child's desires and the world he is forced to live in is conveyed with that unforced skill so characteristic of Trnka's work. The little Emperor is shown waking up in the morning. He jumps out of his little bed, looks into the mirror and, in buoyant mood, paints a moustache under his reflection in the mirror. But he scarcely has time to wipe it off before he must maintain *decorum majestatis*. He slides quickly under his bedclothes as the door opens. The First Minister comes in. He is followed by a strange contraption: a sort of chronometer. It is in the form of a golden tortoise. On its back stands a mechanical jester holding a pair of cymbals between his outstretched hands. Behind appears a procession of courtiers. The chronometer approaches the Emperor's bed. The minister turns a little key. The jester strikes the cymbals. It is time for the *Levée*.

From that moment the contraption becomes master of the Emperor's day. Its strokes impose the rhythm for the morning ceremonial.

A stroke.

The courtiers bring in the toilet necessities and clothes.

A second stroke.

The Emperor washes himself.

A third stroke.

They dress him.

With the same dull-wittedness the chronometer sets the rhythm for the morning walk. At its command the Emperor is permitted to play with the mechanical swans, which float on the glass lake. Even this daily repeated playtime is limited by the chronometer. Relentlessly, the cymbals strike, and relent-lessly, devoid of all feeling, the tortoise continues its mechanical routine.

The few pleasures of the little boy Emperor decrease as he uncovers the secret of his ingenious but dead playthings. He watches a courtier turn the key to set the engine of the toy-swans in motion. Another works the bellows that make the fishes sing.

After introducing the lifeless, not to say deathly, routine of the little Emperor, in which the machine is master of the man, Trnka returns more closely to Hans Andersen's tale. As it unfolds, it becomes clear that Trnka's is not a passive adaptation, but that he has provided a solid background which substantially improves the original idea. In changing it, to convert it into a film, he discovered a broader conception of the theme.

In Andersen's story, the Emperor is reading in his library and he discovers that there is a rare bird he has never heard of living at the edge of his garden. Later he is presented with a mechanical nightingale as a gift from the Emperor of Japan. Trnka joined these two more or less accidental themes by the introduction of a new figure. This was the flying seaman, who lands by balloon in the Emperor's garden. He presents the Emperor with a picture-book of

China, where, among other marvels, the nightingale is depicted. It is he, also, who produces the mechanical bird.

This sailor is a link between the nursery and the fairy tale: he has some of the fleeting qualities of a child's dream. He faintly resembles the characters in Andersen's stories, and in Trnka's book illustrations. His balloon links him to the acted frame: it is no more than an upturned dish suspended in a net beside the bed of the sick boy. With his appearance Trnka launched into the story proper. The sailor is a change or turning-point: for a brief moment reality reappears as the boy rouses himself in his sleep and catches sight of a ball which becomes part of an amusing sequence in the dream.

It provided, in fact, one of the most enchanting scenes in Trnka's film. The Emperor is giving a banquet in honour of the sailor. They sit down at a long table, where there are only chopsticks at the side of each little plate. Little balls of food are set before them, and the Emperor and the courtiers show complete mastery of the chopsticks. But the sailor cannot get a single mouthful into his mouth. The Emperor sends him a little ball from his own plate. He hands it on a chopstick to one of the courtiers, who gives it to his neighbour, and it is handed from chopstick to chopstick down the length of the entire banqueting table. The sailor looks on helplessly. He carefully prods it, tries to lift it, fails, pokes at it again, until the ball rolls from the plate on to the table and from the table down to the floor.

This scene has been criticised for being too protracted, and for being rather a digression on the main theme. But it is redeemed by the poetic charm and gentle humour which infuse a child's confused image of a remote fairyland with a magical playfulness.

In adapting Hans Andersen's story for the puppet film, Trnka had to make the central conflict more pointed, for, unlike the Danish storyteller, he could not rely on words, but had to make the issues clear by means of situation and action. Thus his treatment of the theme is broader. Andersen's tale grew from a central allegory: a comparison between the two singers, the one living, the other artificial. The one touches the human heart, refreshes and strengthens it, by means of its song, without recourse to rules of ceremonies, whereas the other sings the same song over and over again, needs winding before it will sing at all, and performs only when someone is in the mood to listen. In Hans Andersen's tale, one of the courtiers criticises the real nightingale because no one knows what it is going to sing, whereas everything is known beforehand with the artificial bird. It cannot be otherwise than it is: it can be opened up and taken to pieces, and its cylinder and mechanism are something the human mind can understand.

The living nightingale, talking to the Emperor, says of itself:

'I cannot build a nest in the palace and live here, but let me come here when I am in the mood. I am going to sing here to give you joy and give you something to think about. I am going to sing of good and evil, of those things which are kept secret before you . . .'

For five years, Andersen's Emperor enjoyed the song of the mechanical toy before he fell ill, and it was the living nightingale that helped him in his struggle with death. There is no connection between the Emperor's illness and the two birds. 'Five years have passed,' writes Andersen. 'The country is stricken with sorrow . . .'

Trnka's Emperor is taken ill with his longing for the living bird, having been devitalised by the lifeless melody of the mechanical nightingale. This was more than a change arising from transposing the story to turn it into a film-script. It was a totally new conception. Andersen's fairy-tale played down the conflict between the court poets and the free bird. Trnka stressed this theme. He felt the contradiction between the living and mechanical song-birds more acutely than Hans Andersen had done. The way the set was devised, and the lengthy introduction, with the many mechanical toys, emphasises this difference between the two interpretations.

Trnka used the confrontation between the two nightingales as a means of presenting two conceptions of life, and expressing the conflict between reason and emotion, civilisation and culture, mechanicalness and humanity. He was issuing a warning against overstressing the technical aspects of life at the expense of natural, human emotion. He found the old theme of the Hans Andersen tale in key with his own philosophy, and his interpretation gave it a new, living meaning. He retained the symbols, and used them freshly in a deeply-felt story full of poetry.

His conception of the story was shared by Václav Trojan, the composer, who had already shown in *The Czech Year* how ably he could complement Trnka's work. He found musical themes which expressed the contrast between the living and the mechanical nightingale. He gave the toy bird a lifeless song rendered by three mandolines. It was deliberately composed so that it became nerve-racking after repetition. On the other hand, the song of the nightingale, the bird with the living heart, was expressed by a moving violin solo.

Music and picture combined to provide a scene which is poetically the richest and the most beautiful in the film. Towards the end the ailing Emperor reclines on his couch with death sitting at his feet. Death is dressed in black with a top hat, his face covered with a mourning veil. The nightingale's song saddens him; he departs from the Emperor's couch and goes into his garden, the cemetery, where he picks up a small watering can and waters the most precious of his seeds. Then a miracle occurs: from under his watering-can springs up a tombstone. Those who in life knew love or hatred now find reconciliation and eternal friendship. A faithful dog is seen crouching by the side of a little girl; a lover finds his love and rests by her side for ever; soldiers who did not know why they were shooting at each other now clasp each other's hands in friendship.

As the nightingale sings its song, and death waters his seeds, the Emperor becomes well again, and health is restored to the little boy. The crisis has been overcome.

Back in reality, the boy climbs over the fence that had cut him off from the rest of the world and hand in hand with the little girl he runs towards the sun and the grass and the fresh air.

IN *The Emperor's Nightingale* Trnka's style was particularly easy and unforced. He used simple little figures, children's puppets. He made even his old courtier look like a big bad wrinkled child. The straightforward, childlike manner was, of course, deceptive, for the film was subtly expressive of Trnka's serious purpose. For example, the linking of the images between the child's real life and his dream of Hans Andersen's Chinese Emperor's palace showed Trnka's understanding of a child's dream world, while at the same time it expressed his own philosophy, and was an integral part of the story. A crocheted lace pattern reappeared as the design on the porcelain walls of the palace; the flying seaman waved a Czech flag; a little Chinese postillion was travelling in an old-fashioned stage-coach, the design of which was borrowed from the old telegram forms, and the post-horn played a well-known nursery rhyme.

Neither in *The Czech Year* nor in any later

From *The Emperor's Nightingale*

The little girl and the emperor

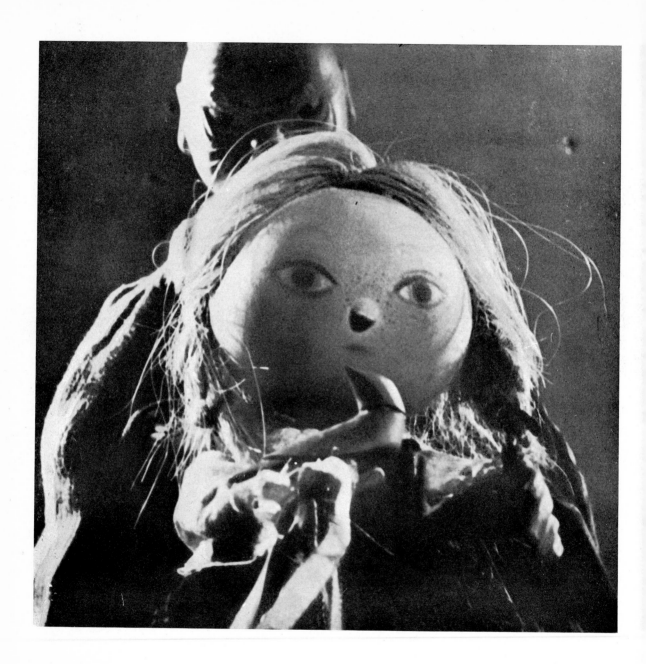

Detail of the little girl

The search for the living nightingale

The astronomer

The frog

Death enters his garden

film did Trnka achieve the perfect unity with the music that made *The Emperor's Nightingale* so wonderfully well integrated. There was no need for words, for the pictures and music together conveyed the full meaning. This, of course, was inherent in the theme, which was about the two forms of music of the two birds. This unity, combined with the well-written story, resulted in a delightful, sunlit film, which, though it was like a child's dream, was really for adults and more easily understood by them. If it had a fault it was that it was too fragile, too gentle, too ingenious, and, for some tastes, too artificial.

Feeling this, perhaps, Trnka followed it with something entirely different in subject matter, spirit and expression.

Three films followed in rapid succession. First came *The Story of the Double-Bass*, to be followed by *The Song of the Prairie* and *The Devil's Mill*.

Expansion of Puppet Acting
Further Puppet Films
The Story of the Double-Bass
The Song of the Prairie
The Devil's Mill

8

FOR TWO YEARS Trnka continued to make full-length puppet films. He acted as his own script-writer and director, designed the sets, and edited the final film. This would have involved an enormous amount of work for one man if they had been ordinary acted films. A puppet film involved even more. The script in itself was a sizeable tome which had to include innumerable illustrations, calcula-tions of timing, indications of movement, and so on. Trnka drew in the script the origi-nal position of every shot, showing its movement with a different coloured pencil, and indicating the movement of each puppet separately from the movement of the camera. The amount of detailed concentration and co-ordination required was immeasurable.

He still found time, however, to develop his technique. *The Czech Year* and *The Empe-ror's Nightingale*, for all the fragility and refinement of expression, in the latter especi-ally, were very primitive in characterisation and animation. The figures lacked individua-lity: they were generalised types or symbols. In *The Czech Year* they represent common national figures. There is the Czech cottager, the game-keeper, the peasant as such. There is no attempt to give them each a personality separate from the type they represent. Their faces are like masks; they have the minimum of personality necessary for plausibility. Only in *Bethlehem* does Trnka deviate from this, and there his puppets are like stage props: they are part of a picture which has been given motion. In *The Emperor's Nightingale* the Chinese Emperor, the first courtier, the sailor, the little girl, the fisherman, are not beings with a life of their own, but symbols in a fairy tale. They serve a different purpose from the puppets in *The Czech Year*, which represent the general concepts of the Czech countryside and folklore. They represent instead two conflicting views of life. The technique, however, was the same. Individual character description was dispensed with, and Trnka concentrated on generalisation.

This was not, of course, a weakness in either film. It was fully intended, and was an integral part of Trnka's treatment. Both films dealt in symbols, and they were conceived from the beginning in this way.

Trnka realised, however, that the approach limited his scope. He knew that as soon as he found a subject which demanded nuances in the rendering of the characters, he would have to make his puppets more individual and precise. It was not only a question of the design of the puppets, but of their capacity for animation. This last was an important factor, for the degree of characterisation corresponded to the degree of animation they were capable of. The mask-like puppets in *The Czech Year* and *The Emperor's Nightingale* express emotion by means of their movements and gestures only, and then in the most general way. At this stage in Trnka's work in films, puppet-acting in the fullest sense scarcely occurs at all: the emotions are expressed in other ways. The only touches of individual characterisation are seen in *The Legend of St. Procopius*, and there is one little figure, an ape-astronomer, in *The Emperor's Nightingale*, who shows distinct characteristics, but these are only rudimentary beginnings.

Trnka therefore set out to enlarge his scope. He embarked upon three shorter films. They represent three experiments and three successes.

THE FIRST of these was *The Story of the Double-Bass*, based on a story by Chekhov. Smychkov, a bass-player, is bathing in a river when a thief makes off with his clothes. He hides in the large case of his double-bass. But inside the case he finds a beautiful young woman, Bibulova, who has met with exactly the same predicament. Smychkov's colleagues, utterly unaware of what has happened, carry the case to the castle where they are to perform, and the girl is revealed in Eve's costume before the astonished and startled company.

The basic situation would be somewhat indecent, were it not for Chekhov's gently humorous, poetic treatment. In transposing it to a film, the same subtlety was necessary, not only to avoid vulgarity, but because the whole charm of the story lay in the discreet treatment of an indiscreet theme. The fact that it was acted by puppets somewhat blunted the edge of any indecency, which would not have been true with living actors. But this would not have been sufficient, had not Trnka stressed the grotesque elements playing up the poetry and comedy, and making his version discreet but in no way prudish. He made sensitive use of curtaining by means of the darkness of the river, and the dark interior of the double-bass case.

Trnka chose this story because he was drawn to Chekhov's gentle, serio-comic humour, and the underlying poetry, which he felt lent itself well to the puppet-film. The story was set between dream and reality, and the characters were already half-puppet and half-human. For this reason, the theme suited Trnka's needs of the moment. Chekhov's characters were not precisely drawn: they were sketches rather than complete people. This gave Trnka an opportunity to test the possibilites of character-drawing in a more precise form than before, without having to launch himself and his animators into the full-scale delineation of individual people.

Thus his two main characters were still generalised but showed some individual features. The girl, a young Countess, was designed as a parody of the nineteenth-century ideal of beauty. Smychkov, the double-bass player, had the expression of an old bachelor, with a drooping moustache, unkempt hair, sad eyes, and a top hat. The effect was most expressive and convincing, though the design and animation of the puppets was better than the general action of the film.

Another very important reason for Trnka's choice was the musical theme of the story. The double-bass had a dramatic role to play. Trnka, still working with Trojan, was keenly aware of the importance of music in helping to express the dramatic theme. In *The Czech Year*, folk songs had provided this. The Czech title of the film, in fact, means a collection of

Countess Bibulova in the *Story of the Double-Bass*

folk songs. In *The Emperor's Nightingale*, the main conflict was expressed by the songs of the two birds. In the two films which followed *The Story of the Double-Bass* there was again a dominant musical theme.

Despite its charm, *The Story of the Double-Bass* betrayed something of its experimental nature: there was evidence of conflict between Trnka's intentions and the ultimate result. For the first time, he did not rely solely on music and the visual effect of his puppets, but had a spoken commentary. He began to make greater demands on each puppet, and to seek for new possibilities in the puppet film.

HE FOUND an entirely new genre in his next film, *The Song of the Prairie*. In *The Story of the Double-Bass*, he had shown himself as a humorist capable of arousing a melacholy smile. In *The Song of the Prairie* he revealed his

gifts as a comedian, with the power to make the audience laugh aloud.

The story is set in a world entirely different from that of Chekhov's fateful *soirée*. This is the Wild West, the country of the superman, where the pistol is cocked and ready at all

A surprise at a Musical Soirée in *The Story of the Double-Bass*

time, and there is no room for timidity. Love blossoms at first sight.

For this film, Trnka did not write his own script. J. Brdečka, the script-writer, took his inspiration from one of the earliest Wild West classics. He kept closely to all the rules of the game, particularly in the dramatic build-up. He created a hero who was the essence of all the manly virtues, an outstanding horseman, an unsurpassed shot, knowing no hesitation or faltering. Confronting him was the villain, a gambler, a cynical seducer of women, and leader of a band of robbers: in short, the embodiment of vice. Between them was a case of gold, and, of course, a woman, as beautiful as she was innocent, and losing her heart to the hero at first sight.

Trnka was not new to the art of parody. His first independent effort in the puppet theatre had been a parody on the sentimental seafaring story, *The Merman*. When he turned to animated cartoons, *The Gift*, one of his most important achievements, was again basically a parody. It is worth recalling *The Gift* in connection with *The Song of the Prairie*, because in both the script-writer uncovered for Trnka new possibilities in expression through puppets. Both had movement, rhythm, a definite dramatic situation, and a rapid turn of events. The spate of events in *The Song of the Prairie* never ceased. Action followed upon action, events flying ahead to the rhythm set by the beat of the hooves of the six horses drawing the stage-coach.

Again there was a strong musical theme, provided by the hero's 'hill-billy' song. This was one of the few films where Trnka did not work with Trojan: the music was composed by J. Rychlík. Trnka, Brdečka and Rychlík made no secret of the fact that they had borrowed the plot. Since this was a parody it in no way weakened the effect. In fact, the ready-made story enabled them to concentrate on ideas and gimmicks which would underline the absurdities of the tradition of the Western. It gave Trnka the opportunity he was seeking for developing his characterisation, and from this point of view *The Song of the Prairie* was important. It gave Trnka and his animators valuable experience. Parody is a special type of caricature, giving scope for exaggerated characterisation and over-emphasis of single traits. There are few better opportunities for experiment. The style and the *genre* were made for it.

Trnka sharply contrasted the two main puppets, the hero and the villain. The hero was blue-eyed, fair-haired with an expression of besotted handsomeness. The villain was

Characters in *The Song of the Prairie*

Trnka caricatures himself in
the figure of the Mail Coach Guard

The Villain and his horse

The Hero

dark, of course, with a clipped moustache and deep-set burning black eyes. He had the elongated face of a decadent. The woman had the Rossetti-type of beauty, somewhat reminiscent of Countess Bibulova in *The Story of the Double-Bass*. Several other clear-cut figures were grouped around these types, all visualised and defined with clarity.

These included the driver of the stage-coach, with a terrible squint and a pipe, and the stout guard of the mail-coach, who emptied bottle after bottle at a draught. His eyes and big mousy-coloured moustache were reminiscent of Trnka himself, who probably intended this figure as a caricature of himself.

The difference in the design of the puppets was paralleled by a difference in the animation. It was no longer merely a question of expressing simple emotions by means of movement. The puppets were really beginning to act. Trnka used his blond hero amusingly in one sequence to underline the absurd convention which enables the hero of a cowboy film to retain his well groomed appearance, and to have complete mastery of every unpleasant situation. The villain hurls a boulder at the blond head of the hero, who responds by taking out a pocket mirror and straightening his parting. He walks with light ballet-steps, while the villain has to crawl on all fours to prevent himself from falling.

There was as yet no complex psychology, but the difference in design and animation, as compared with *The Czech Year* and *The Emperor's Nightingale*, was noticeable.

IN HIS THIRD FILM, *The Devil's Mill*, Trnka attempted something entirely different. After the serio-comedy based on a Russian classic, and the parody of the American Western, came a story of Czech origin. At first glance, it might seem that Trnka had

returned to the genre of *The Czech Year*. It is as though the veteran soldier who appeared in *The Village Feast* sequence of *The Czech Year* had been rejuvenated to take the central rôle in this ghost story. But Trnka had moved too far from *The Czech Year* for this to be more than a coincidence. The similarity was due solely to the Czech atmosphere and subject. Basically *The Devil's Mill* was something quite new and independent.

Again, the theme had music at its core. An old, one-legged veteran soldier is touring the countryside, a barrel-organ over his shoulder. Every so often he turns the wheel to beg for a slice of bread. But as soon as the tinny music issues forth, the people close their windows and the animals run away, until, late one evening, a little boy takes pity on him and gives him a slice of bread. And just as he is about to eat it to still his hunger, a silver-haired old man — a real fairy-tale figure — appears before him and asks if he can share his meal. The organ-grinder agrees, and in return for this kindness, the old man gives him a new handle for his barrel organ. It has magic power, and as soon as he begins to turn it, a merry polka sounds which no one can resist, and everybody feels an urge to dance.

In the evening, tired out, the organ-grinder is attracted by the brightly-lit windows of a deserted mill. Inside the table is laid and everything is prepared for guests. There are buns, roast goose, mugs of beer, even a tin of tobacco. And a bed is made on top of the tiled stove. The old soldier falls to and eats the food, and then retires to bed.

At midnight the objects in the room suddenly come to life. The old man's nightshirt slips off, and the featherbed disappears through the door. These events herald the appearance of the instigator of them: the devil himself, who suddenly appears through the door. But the old soldier knows no fear and begins to fight him. He is really hard pressed, when, at the last moment, he is saved by his barrel-organ and its magic handle. Not even the devil can resist the polka. He is compelled to dance until his time is up . . .

After this eerie night, the old soldier refills the mill-stream to set the mill-wheels turning, and puts on a miller's cap. The merry sound of the mill-wheels echoes round the countryside.

In this film, Trnka returned to his earlier style of puppet design and animation. The animation was much simpler than in the two previous short films, precise character draw-

The veteran in *The Devil's Mill*

From *The Devil's Mill*

ing was not attempted, and the acting of the puppets was reduced to a minimum. But other elements were emphasised. Trnka approached the film as an illustrator. He had drawn veteran soldiers, dragoons, and devils of all sorts, large and small, innumerable times in his children's books. As he had no problems with design, he could concentrate fully on the direction, and on the sound effects, which he made into an important feature. Trojan was again composing for him, and for the first time, real sounds were used to complement his music. During the old soldier's night in the mill there are continual noises, creating an effect of terror and ghostliness. The floor creaks, there is a knocking on the ceiling, there is whining down the chimney, squeaks, buzzes, screams outside the window. As the clock strikes the witching hour, the noises reach a crescendo and an unbelievable hullabaloo breaks out, followed by a tense silence. And then, from the ceiling drop hands, head, and limbs, and out of these parts, with a chuckle, emerges the devil in person. Added to the new device of sound effects, was the animation of the objects in the room, such as the nightshirt, the featherbed, the chair, table and broom.

DESPITE the difference in material and expression, *The Story of the Double-Bass*, *The Song of the Prairie*, and *The Devil's Mill* are clearly interlinked. They could be regarded as a humorous triptych, showing three different aspects of Trnka's comic vision. *The Story of the Double-Bass* represents laughter tinged with melancholy; *The Song of the Prairie* robust laughter at absurdity; and *The Devil's Mill* secret, inner laughter at the grotesque. Each film, too, had its own poetry, linked to the laughter it provoked.

The three films are linked, too, for the technical experience Trnka gained through them. He tested the possibilities of characterisation of a subtler kind than in *The Czech Year* or *The Emperor's Nightingale*. He tried the effect of using real sound and words as well as music, and he explored the possibilities of more advanced character acting by puppets. Original in themselves, the three films were also important in Trnka's development, for they were his preparation for a full-length film to come. In it Trnka was to link all his new discoveries.

9

AT THE BEGINNING of 1949, Trnka began work on his third full-length film. While he was in the course of shooting it, his studio moved to new premises, in a former cinema. It was not ideal, but more suitable than the premises they had left. The former auditorium was adapted to make several separate studios. Right at the back was a small cubby-hole, with an office desk and some chairs. This was turned into Trnka's holy of holies, and it served this purpose for many years to come.

The mood of *The Czech Year* was lyrical, that of *The Emperor's Nightingale* symbolic. Trnka was now determined to tell a story in the epic mood. He found the subject in two fairy stories by a well-known Czech woman writer Božena Němcová. They were called *Prince Bayaya* and *The Magic Sword*. Trnka used the name of the hero alone for his film: *Bayaya*. In his version Bayaya was no prince but a poor country lad, who at the end returned with his bride to the cottage where he was born to serve his ageing father. This was typical of the adaptations he made. He saw the folk tale hero as an embodiment of popular ideas of honour, courage and morality,

but as folk tales had acquired certain irrelevant or contradictory trappings through the time at which they had arisen, he accepted the poetry and magic of the fairy tale, but adapted it accordingly.

The film opens with a decorative title, faintly reminiscent of a beautiful illustration in an illuminated book. This takes the spectator back into the fairy-tale period, and symbolises the literary background of the film, like the dropping of the book of Hans Andersen's Fairy Tales in *The Emperor's Nightingale*. The mysterious atmosphere deepens when an owl is shown perched on a cottage roof, and a child's voice is heard singing solo the first words of a well-known song:

Once upon a time there was a son,
Who lived with his father, a modest man,
They lived in a cottage poor and small,
They watched the shadows on it fall.

This brief introduction takes us at once into the fairy-tale world, where magical events take place. The sad, ballad-like mood presages the great struggle the hero will

Bayaya (scenario and realisation)

137

have to face. The first sequence produces a strange inner tension.

Bayaya's father, an old man, is waiting for him at the table; they have their meal and go to bed. The father drops off to sleep at once, the son tosses about sleepless. He seems

turns back again. Bayaya looks into its eyes. The horse addresses him in a human voice:

'I am your Mother, and this is my purgatory. If you want to set me free and be happy yourself, mount on my saddle; I will carry you away from here . . .'

to have a sense of foreboding; something, he knows not what, is going to happen. At that moment a white horse appears at the cottage window. It approaches, runs off, and then

After this prologue the second part is introduced with a written sub-title again, and a child's song. Bayaya is shown setting off on the horse towards a distant castle; he

Bayaya (scenario and realisation)

Bayaya and the princess

The suitors in *Bayaya*

tethers the mare on a rocky cliff and enlists for royal service.

Then a new part is introduced, as before. This is to take the spectator into the environment of the castle, where the innocent princesses frolic with Bayaya, and where the king and his jester are sadly awaiting the inexorable visit of three dragons to whom the princesses have been pledged.

The expected evil comes true: the monsters settle in the black lake outside the town. The great dramatic moment has arrived, towards which the story has been relentlessly moving.

The eldest of the princesses is the first to be sacrificed. Bayaya departs secretly from the castle, and clad in armour provided by his mother he overpowers the dragon. And so with the second and the third.

Trnka had never before handled such a dramatic episode as Bayaya's duel with the dragon. Unfortunately, it was here, at the moment of climax in the film, that Trnka failed to achieve dramatic impact. In the prose text, the three fights, in the tradition of fairy tales, are exactly the same. This serves to mark each step in the story. But in the film this repetition is irritating in its effect. The fact that Trnka remained faithful to the fairy-tale rules and reproduced the same situation three times over prevented him from developing any one of them dramatically, and he had merely to rest content with suggesting this each time.

The next act has a new prologue. The hero has dragged the princesses out of the clutches of the monsters, but he has still managed to remain incognito. The king now wishes to marry off his daughters, and he invites suitors to come from far and wide. Each one of the noble suitors is introduced, and at this point Trnka leaves the fairy-tale world, and enters quite different territory. The story becomes for a time a parody of feudalism. The degenerateness of one suitor is emphasised, the senility of another, the bad temper of the third, the stupid brutality of the fourth.

The princesses have to roll apples, their suitors being chosen by the direction the apples take. They all roll to Bayaya's feet. He avoids the apple of the older sisters, and picks up the one thrown by the youngest princess. The reaction of the knights, the princesses and the king far exceed the demands of the fairy tale, which were simply: 'the proud princesses turned up their noses at the poor bridegroom'. Trnka made the scene into a head-on encounter between two worlds and two classes. The princess rejects Bayaya. The noblemen are in a rage. And

2

Tři princezny si
házejí míčem
prostřední ze zády
ostatní tři si vyměňí
míč
pak se one zpět
evně princezna chytí
míč nahoru zpět míč
střih v letu

1

první princ. drží míč zaráží se hledí dolů po chvíli pomalu pozdí švenk s míčem ukaže 1 dolů	druhá chytí míč volně se ahlédne dolů švenk → 2	Třetí princ. se naklání s balkonu ostatní přijdou nahý- bají se přes 3

strhaný Bzoza
stojí pod hradem
zpívá hlubou
se ukloní a
zpívá dál

hroze na loutnu

černá vodu
míč spadne
na zem

Bayaya (scenario and realisation)

The king with his daughters in *Bayaya*

the wise jester, who had welcomed Bayaya's good luck with applause, is cruelly punished by one of the other suitors.

In the next sequence Trnka carried on his satire on feudalism. It is introduced by a rousing drinking song:

The Squire had his fun,
His head askew,
Oh, the damage he has done,
Everything's got to be new.

The song underlines the common man's view of the 'fun' of his 'betters'. Trnka's satire was stronger than the parody in *The Song of the Prairie*.

The scene changes to a tournament. Trnka still has his tongue in his cheek, as the horses of the heavily armed riders are shown in careful detail, with all their trappings. The lords are shown tilting in the tournament, and the victor is the stupidest of the suitors, Trnka's satire of a 'he-man'. Then Bayaya rides on to the scene, and with a single stroke overpowers him. The defeated knight falls off his horse, saddle and all.

The story moves to the close. The victorious Bayaya refuses the laurels offered him by the princess who had rejected him previously. This is his punishment for her, which starts a new thread in the story. There now follow several parallel events: the eldest princess celebrates her wedding. The jester takes his revenge for his previous debasement, a minstrel, a magician, and a singer come to entertain the wedding guests. The youngest princess is sad, because of the quarrel with Bayaya. But in the end Bayaya sets his mother's spirit free, and finally finds and makes his peace with the Princess.

In *Bayaya* Trnka tried to achieve a synthesis of all the media of expression he had used previously in his films. In *The Czech Year*, song had accompanied the pictures almost continuously. Now it was used for a different purpose: a song introduced each section of the story. He had used spoken words in the form of a commentary for the first time in *The Story of the Double-Bass*. Now he again made use of the spoken word.

Bayaya, however, marked a transition for Trnka. No other film has so many contradictory elements. The forces were arrayed for a radical change, but this had not yet taken place. The style of expression was already new, but the working out of the drama did not yet match it. It was as though the work of the designer and producer foretold a new style, more dramatic and truly psychological than the poetic style of the first two films. But the dramatic content of the film was unequal to the new demands. Puppets can in fact act tragedy or comedy, but here the script-writer did not give them the chance to do so. As a dramatist, Trnka did not fully understand all the possibilities open to the producer, or make use of them. His interpretation of the story lacked a strong, properly developed central theme. Where the situation seemed to demand drama, he was inclined to lapse into a lyrical or epic mood. And he did not attempt to eliminate the many threads of the story, and make a concentrated dramatic theme. Instead, he left it diffuse.

In the same way, he failed to achieve unity

of style. The first part of the film was a typical folk story, with a simple hero, a careworn royal father, a mother under a spell. But the second part was closer in spirit to a more sophisticated Renaissance comedy, in which the fairy-tale aspects contrast sharply with the rest. The atmosphere is jovial, and the jester would only need to relate some anecdote jibing at the feudal lords to make us think that we were watching a Shakespearean play.

The disharmony between the parts produced a total effect which was not properly integrated. There was insufficient

Jester in *Bayaya*

dramatic tension, and the slow-moving story did not hold the spectators' attention. On the other hand, some of the details remain unforgettable. The film is full of poetic enchantment. In spite of all its shortcomings, *Bayaya* stands as the work of a great artist.

Although the film as a whole lacked dramatic impact, Trnka achieved new success with the acting of his puppets in certain scenes in *Bayaya*. In *The Story of the Double-Bass* and *The Song of the Prairie*, animation was just beginning to turn into real puppet-acting. He successfully carried this a stage further in *Bayaya*. Character, for the first time, was expressed with precision, and portrayed gently but decisively. The scenes, where the jester soothed the princess, or applauded Bayaya's victory over the suitors were masterly solos of acting with puppets. Bayaya himself was less effective, though he had some remarkable moments, as did the king. The sensitive portrayal of character showed that Trnka and his team were ready for more exacting tasks in this field.

The décor of *Bayaya* was a work of art in itself. Trnka drew his inspiration from Gothic and early Renaissance painting: mainly from the work of Czech illuminators. But he adapted freely, making no attempt to copy a certain period in art, but turning it all into an original fairy-tale world. It was timeless, free of conventions. He contented himself with faint echoes, rather than an excess of descriptiveness: a column, gobelin tapestry or niche would suggest a castle hall.

TRNKA himself regarded *Bayaya* as a turning-point in his development. He had reached a stage where his work as a puppet-film director was to move off in a different direction.

There had already been indications that he would embark on something entirely new. Now it became inevitable, for otherwise his work would merely have demonstrated that the puppet-film was a limited medium, and could not proceed past the point where drama, firmly conceived and based on precise drawing, began. It would seem that he had exhausted all the possibilities of the medium in his previous work. His next achievement was to be decisive not only for Trnka himself, but for the future of the puppet film. There were only two possibilities: either he had to repeat himself, or to break down the limits he had reached in *Bayaya*. He had either to gain complete mastery of the medium, and demonstrate that the puppet could convey the maximum impression of humanity, or he must resign himself to the stiffness of the dolls, and return to the symbol.

Trnka had never been so clearly aware of the importance of his next step. For when he had made *The Czech Year*, he had been carried along with enthusiasm, because he had finally found a medium that used his puppets. Everything had been new, and he had been able to approach his task with freshness. Now he had to find his second wind. Further progress seemed impossible, and yet he knew that he must make it, or he had reached a static point. For more than a year he carried out experiments unconnected with puppet films.

And then, in the autumn of 1951, a news item appeared in the Press, stating that Trnka was working on the script of a new full-length film. It was to be based on the cycle of *Legends of Old Bohemia*, as recorded by Cosmas and A. Jirásek.

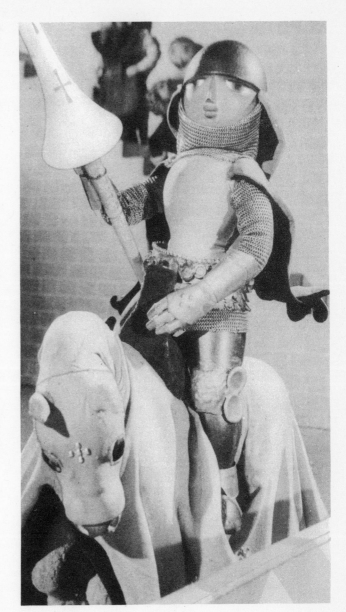

Bayaya

IO

IT WAS NOT only the problems of the work itself that made Trnka pause for a year and occupy himself with minor short films. There were several reasons, and amongst them was the need to relax after the exhausting work on *Bayaya*. Trnka also wanted to take his time before launching into a experiment that would answer some of the critics who had cast doubts upon his work. Although *The Czech Year* had been so enthusiastically received by the critics there had been a few isolated voices from those who had a blind spot for Trnka. Their adverse comments had provoked little reaction, but they had sown the seeds of a misunderstanding about his work. On the first night of *The Emperor's Nightingale* these seeds were shown to have fallen on fertile ground. Controversy raged round the film, and continued when Trnka produced *The Story of the Double-Bass, The Song of the Prairie*, and *The Devil's Mill*. Trnka was accused of formalism, of a tendency to *art pour l'art*, cosmopolitanism, and a host of other artistic sins. But mainly the critics objected to the fact that his films were unsuitable for children. They said that *The Story of the Double-Bass*, for instance, was too sophisticated, and that *The Devil's Mill* was too frightening.

This was the core of the misunderstanding that grew up around Trnka as time went on. In fact, Trnka had not intended his films for children. From the very beginning Trnka wished to attract adult audiences to the puppet film. *The Czech Year* and the films that followed it were intended for adults. Trnka believed the puppet capable of expressing important emotions and ideas. This had been true of the puppet theatre when it was at its height: it had become entertainment for children only when it had become decadent as an art form, and this had caused a prejudice which faced anyone who tried to revive it as a serious medium of expression. Trnka, in the direct line of puppetry tradition, had to wage the same struggle to claim the serious attention of the adult spectator as his teachers in the puppet theatre had done. He met repeatedly with prejudice against puppets, in the minds of people who thought they could only perform simple tales for little children. Trnka himself, of course, did not under-estimate art designed for children. He had himself achieved a great deal in this line, with his children's book illustrations. But his puppet films had a different aim.

Bayaya clarified the matter, and cleared the air of misunderstanding. The critics made their peace with Trnka, the film was awarded a national film prize, and the hostile voices were silent.

Trnka was determined, however, to give an even more convincing answer in his next film. This was to be something entirely new: an experiment that needed to be understood. It was a difficult step to take, and for that reason he hesitated.

THE RESULT of this interim period was three short films. Two of them, *The Golden Fish* and *How Grandpa Changed till Nothing was Left*, are excursions back into the world of animated cartoons. The effect was achieved by means of static drawing and the movements and cuts of the camera. The third film, *The Happy Circus*, was an experiment in bringing paper figures to life.

The Golden Fish was the best of the fairy stories, largely due to the witty commentary spoken by the popular actor Jan Werich. Trnka used many original ideas to create a pleasing and interesting spectacle. It was a tale of greediness punished, in which he enlivened the telling with a cascade of tiny absurdities in pictures and words. It had an unforgettable charm.

The same cannot be said of the other film, *How Grandpa Changed till Nothing was Left.* Here the words were predominant, and the story could easily have existed without Trnka's drawings, which simply illustrated the story.

The Golden Fish

But *The Happy Circus* was very successful, both as a film and a work of art. Trnka invited three leading painters and illustrators to collaborate with him: František Tichý, Kamil Lhoták and Zdeněk Seydl. The film consisted of circus numbers strung loosely together, each one containing new ideas and novel tricks. It was an exercise in entertainment by means of animation, and its sole purpose was to amuse and surprise the audience. It achieved this superbly: there was not a flaw to be found in the style or execution.

At this time Trnka was also collaborating on several other films, which included *The Gingerbread Cottage* and *Kuťásek and Kutilka*.

Trnka had now begun to visualise some of the individual shots in his own new puppet film. Gradually, as the mental images assumed concrete form, the time came to set aside his minor work.

From the depths of the long remembered past there emerged before Trnka's eyes the forms of warriors and heroes, characters whose deeds had been preserved and embodied in the myths as a lesson to later generations.

He hesitated no longer: a new struggle was about to begin.

The Happy Circus

The arrival on Mount Říp   The drawing of Forefather Czech in the scenario of *Old Czech Legends*

Old Czech Legends
Sources
Adaptation
Speech Introduced
Action and Direction
Puppets developed as Individuals

II

IT IS IMPOSSIBLE for an art historian to do more than evaluate and describe what an artist creates, outline the circumstances that led to it, make comparisons with other artists, and leave it to the sensitivity of the reader to guess at the artist's inner struggle.

In selecting the legends of his people, Trnka was dealing with a subject on the borders of history and mythology, which had been passed on and altered through generations, and contained a people's innermost philosophy. Film producers had tried more than once to deal with material of this kind. They had never been successful, except for Eisenstein, in his *Alexander Nevsky*. In all the others, the myths had turned into masquerade, the dignified stories into carnival. It is small wonder that Trnka's intention raised doubts in people's minds. Famous directors

who had failed over similar subjects had relied on the skill of stars as famous as themselves. Trnka had only his puppets. Nothing seemed more remote from their tiny world than the grandeur of the myths. It seemed most unlikely that the delicate wooden figures would be able to capture the heroic quality of the ancient legends.

But was Trnka right? He believed that the mask-like faces of his puppets would preserve the magic spell of the myths. *The Legend of St. Procopius* had, after all, shown something of what Trnka had in mind. There was no ready answer to that question, nor to the many others posed by the new venture.

One problem was the plot of the film. Trnka invited two writers to help him with the script. They had two sources. One was a group of six stories from the cycle *Legends of Old Bohemia*, collected and retold by Alois Jirásek (an English version, with Trnka's illustrations, was published in 1963). The other was the Chronicle of Cosmas, a monk of the second half of the 11th century, who had made the first written record of the history of the first Czech thanes, which even then had partly entered the realms of legend. Fragments and outlines of actual events still existed, but the rest had vanished in the depth of the prehistoric era. Whereas a prose story can bridge gaps with brief synopses, without this being regarded as a fault, a film plot cannot afford to do so. Trnka and his script-writers were involved in inventing and adding, to fill in where the events were virtually unknown. More than this, it was essential to try to delve into the minds of people who lived in long distant ages, and to imagine their behaviour, their thoughts and their passions.

The choice of this subject showed the courage and confidence Trnka now felt, despite the doubts and scepticism of other people. His strong feeling for popular forms of expression had guided him well when he made *The Czech Year*, and it helped him now. But the subject was quite different: the artist and lyricist now had to make way for the dramatist and ballad-singer. Sweetness and charm were to be replaced by sharp outlines, and an heraldic effect. Playfulness had no place in this world of sad deliberation and rough passion. But the link between the country and its people was there, as it had been in *The Czech Year*, and it was for Trnka to attempt to give it a new form.

AND SO CAME TRNKA'S new big film: *Old Czech Legends*. This was the story of his forefathers, brought back from the depths of the remote ages to encourage the men of his own day.

Out of the mists beyond time and space sound the notes of a mysterious lyre, introducing an ancient story. The voice of the bard is heard:

'Harken to the legends of ancient days, to the stories of our ancestors, our forefathers, who came into our country and settled along the Rivers Labe (Elbe) and Vltava.'

The first legend, *The Legend of Forefather Czech*, rapidly unfolds.

A puppet appears, its countenance a sad mask. It raises its hands. A sorrowful cry is heard: 'You were our chieftain, you were our father...' Forefather Czech is dead. His body is lying on a funeral pyre about to be kindled. Around it can be heard the songs of mourning... Above the dead man's head sits a grey falcon, the symbol of a great life.

The burial ritual is a frame for the story proper, which describes Forefather Czech's life and deeds in flash-backs. It shows his arduous wanderings as he travelled westward in search of a new country, and the symbolic scene on Mount Říp where the country received its name. Then the new settlers are seen in their struggle against nature, felling trees, building huts, hunting and fishing, tilling the soil. They contend with the mysterious and inexplicable elements, and whenever support is needed, they seek the pure and wise counsel of the chieftain. When the weak sink beneath the strain of the march, he helps them. When lightning burns down the settlement and the panic-stricken people fall on their knees before the anger of the gods, he gives orders to pick up the drinking gourds and pour water on the flames.

But his days are numbered like everyone else's. And just as one day the over-ripe apples drop off the tree, the old man expires. The burial scene is shown once more. The princess sets fire to the funeral pyre. The grey falcon flutters heavenwards ...

The Legend of Forefather Czech was in the epic style. Its themes were man and nature, and man and his country. It was typically Slavonic in feeling. There were several moments which recalled *The Czech Year*, among them the meeting of the bag-piper and the water nymph.

The very first shots showed the radical change in Trnka's style. Between *The Czech Year* and *Bayaya*, Trnka's progress had been gradual. Now the change was more drastic. The puppets themselves were much more expressive. In addition, the main medium of expression was no longer a combination of music and pictures. Words and real sounds predominated. *Old Czech Legends* was the first film in which the puppets actually spoke. Nothing had worried Trnka so much as the idea of a puppet that spoke: he felt that the static masks of the figures would be incongruous combined with speech, which necessitated a moving face. But the subject cried out for speech, and he therefore devised different methods by which the difficulty could be overcome. In *The Legend of Forefather Czech* he used voices in the manner of a chorus, to express the sufferings of the little community in the form of lamentation. The scene at the burial of Forefather Czech is typical of his new use of sound. The emotional tone is set by voices speaking in sad, yet heroic pathos to a background of sound. A monotonous, repetitive wailing establishes the mood: after a while the chorus takes up the words and repeats them in a chant. Trojan's music had by no means lost its significance, but now it had to take the words into account, and contribute with them to unity of expression.

In *The Legend of Bivoj* one of the figures actually spoke, the voice being that of the well-known actor V. Vydra. It was linked to the preceding legend by the words of the bard and the music, which was played on a lyre by the bard to accompany the new tale. In order to link the voice with the puppet, without destroying the effect the puppets produced, Trnka contrived that the speaker should appear only in outline, full attention being turned on those he addressed.

With a gesture the old man indicates that he wishes to speak. The actual speech begins with an exclamation to claim the listeners' attention, and at that sound the camera shows the puppet with his mouth wide open. 'Worthy brethren, hear my speech and do not take it lightly...' the camera quickly retreats and shows the panorama of the hall through which the beautifully stylised voice re-echoes.

The bard goes on to tell of the wild boar which is menacing the people of the countryside around the Wild Boar Hills, threatening the huntsmen and the ploughmen in the fields. He turns to the young men with an appeal: 'Ah, you who are brave, tell me, ah, where the strong huntsmen are, tell me, where...'

The warrior with the falcon in *Old Czech Legends*

Krok's daughters in *Old Czech Legends*

The blind bard (scenario and realisation)
in *Old Czech Legends*

The young men hang their heads in shame. The last, unfinished 'where' expresses the old man's resignation. The scene, a prologue to the actual story, ends as it began. At the closing words, the camera gives a detailed shot of the old minstrel, who makes a mighty gesture to emphasise his challenge. Then the camera again shows the reaction of the listeners. At last the hero of the legend, Bivoj, appears.

There is a sudden change of scene, and we are in the region below the Wild Boar Hills. It is snowing. Bivoj, spear in hand, is walking through the snow. He is singing an old Czech song. Its tune forms the main theme of the legend. It might seem from this that Trnka and Trojan had returned to the manner of *The Czech Year* in the use of song. But here it played an entirely different part: its purpose was not poetic, but dramatic. It recurs several times, each time with a different dramatic purpose. At first it sounds carefree, at ease, playful. The merry tune is in sharp contrast with the deed the young hero is to undertake, as he ploughs through the snow following the wild boar's track. This creates a kind of tension between the puppet and the sound, a counterpoint of picture and music which is intensely nerve-racking. At the moment when Bivoj catches sight of the wild boar, the song ceases. Bivoj simply repeats the last words mechanically.

Trnka makes Bivoj defeat the boar as much by resource and ingenuity as by physical strength. He blinds the animal with a handful of snow, and just at the moment when it is helpless he seizes it and throws it over his shoulder. The fight sequence is a culminating point in the animation and direction. Bivoj stiffens for just a fraction of a second when he first catches sight of the boar. He stands motionless, tightening the grip on the spear in his hand. Then he grunts slightly, picks up a handful of snow and hurls it at the boar. All this is shown in a sequence of details, tiny points perfectly observed and depicted with mastery.

The song returns. In one sequence it is sung by a chorus of dancers, softly, almost indifferently, without passion. In the great hall it sounds for the last time, in honour of the victor, as Bivoj kills the boar with his spear. But this is a very different sound from the preceding chorus. Now the song is joyful, passionate, full of exaltation, with a strong erotic flavour.

The Legend of Bivoj shows the style of the whole film at its best. In it, Trnka achieved a remarkable unity of picture, movement, word and music. He used real sounds

Bivoj brings the boar to Vyšehrad Castle
in *Old Czech Legends*

Libuše,
messengers sent to Přemysl,
and detail of Přemysl
in *Old Czech Legends*

On the following page:
Ploughing (scenario and realisation) in *Old Czech Legends*

hra

radlice vyrývá
hlínu
(smýchá dřívou
zem a sochavištěou hlínu

jedene s ní
ohořelé větve
v cestě

vytrhne !
kočáru

t₁ — STS

prší
dvě krávy táhnou
pluh
(srovny pro-
mitmuty neostře
nehné šedé
muž se dře
při zemi mlha
radlice narazí
vali, marně Tat
noji zastaví el
muž se narovná
hledí dolů na

STS radlice zaražená
o balvan muž
klekne na jedno
koleno ponoří ruce
do hlíny pod balvan
a táhne hlovu přitiskne
až k balvanu Tahne
balvan pomalu povo-
luje hlína
hr STS
se advaluje

STS

staví é vody
9

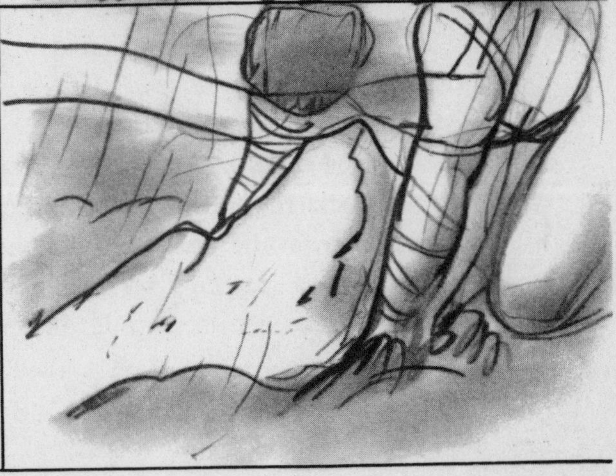

in a masterly fashion, and even the symbolic movement of objects, used in *The Czech Year* and *The Emperor's Nightingale*, was used again here, in order to supplement the actions of the puppet by means of suggestion.

When, for example, Bivoj kills the wild boar the entourage cheer. Trnka stresses the spontaneous enthusiasm which seizes everyone by means of a few brief shots of the ceiling of the great hall. An axe pierces the wooden panelling. Then a spear, then another, then a third, a tenth. The hollow sound of metal on wood mingles with the beginning of a dance tune. The warriors cast away their weapons to dance.

The Legend of Bivoj does not have the depth of *The Legend of Forefather Czech*, but it has strength, a concentrated theme, and dramatic unity and a careful balance. It was one of the high spots of the cycle.

The third legend was symbolic, its ideas embodying the central theme of the whole cycle. *The Legend of Bivoj* celebrated the hero: the individual. *The Legend of Přemysl the Ploughman* was the saga of the founder of the dynasty of Přemyslids, and it celebrated the tradition associated with a national leader who was drawn from the people. Again the story was set in a frame. Two brothers, Chrudoš and Šťáhlav, are in dispute over a field boundary. The scene is a court, presided over by the Princess Libuše. Chrudoš refuses to accept the Princess's decision, and so she goes to the sacred grove to consult the gods, who advise her to call upon Přemysl. Přemysl, a simple ploughman, brings his rope sandals with him when he is called upon to sit at the Princess's table. These are a symbol, meant to remind his descendants that the founder of this dynasty came from among the people and from behind a plough.

It might seem difficult to reconcile Přemysl's saying 'I came from among the people, they are my equals', with his other pronouncement: 'I shall rule over you with a rod of iron.' It is outside the scope of this book to examine how far Trnka imposed his own views on his characters: to what extent he had placed these views in Přemysl's mouth, or how far they were the expression of a people's dreams and longings, embodied in the legendary figure of Přemysl, and uttered by him. We can be sure, however, that Trnka wished to relate his theme to the present, and to give new meaning to the notion of firm government by the people and for the people.

In its manner of expression, *The Legend of Přemysl* was close to *The Legend of Forefather Czech*. Poetical sketches and symbols merged with more dramatic passages, with story-telling in the epic manner, and with lyrical interludes. One of the most attractive passages was Libuše's walk to the sacred glade. The puppet of Přemysl was highly successful in design. Trnka gave it a dramatic expression to balance the impressive tone of voice.

The Legend of Přemysl was somewhat marred in its total effect by the fact that it overlapped with the next legend, which was *The Legend of the Women's War*.

This legend, as it appears in Trnka's sources, had complex ideas behind it. Jirásek's version of the women's war painted an almost sinister picture of a bitter war of women against men, ending with the young thane Ctirad being broken on the wheel, and the rebellion of the women being drowned in blood. Anything of the kind was alien to Trnka, who kept closer to Cosmas' version, which ends in a truce, the victory of healthy love. But his treatment was more intimate than either, and he altered Cosmas' version freely. He imbued it with the robust emotions of real men, giving it almost a Renaissance spirit. At times the relationship between the two central characters evokes Shakespeare: Šárka and Ctirad have a pretended antagonism which cannot fully suppress their natural attraction for each other. Trnka's

version does not show that the original legend reflected a serious change in the organisation of ancient society, the transition from matriarchy to patriarchy. Trnka was not concerned with turning to old patterns, but with using history to speak to his contemporaries. In his version the legend ends, not with the subordination of the women, but with the dance of love of two equal sexes.

The story is linked to *The Legend of Přemysl the Ploughman* by the characters of Libuše and Přemysl. The rule of the women had prevailed until the arrival of Přemysl at Vyšehrad Castle. The disgruntled maidens of Libuše's retinue set off to build themselves a castle on the opposite rocky bank, and to live without men. Trnka, from the beginning, adopts a slight tone of ridicule which makes the legend more human, without departing from the context. He shows his meaning, and sets the mood by a brief introduction, where a young thane, Ctirad, offers Vlasta, the leader of the group of maidens, a spindle to indicate to her that she should take to weaving, not to the sword. He uses the bard to clarify the meaning of several scenes, and the story unfolds, told with obvious delight and a liking for grotesque detail.

On a hot summer day, Ctirad sets off from

Vyšehrad Castle for his native village, escorted by a knight. Somewhere in the distance a shepherd's pipe sounds. Everything is quiet. Only the accompanying tune sounds a warning and introduces into the picture a slight premonition of eroticism and sensuality. Before the eyes of the riders there is revealed a beautiful girl bound with rope to a tree-trunk. Beside her is a large jar of mead.

In the scene which follows, Trnka demonstrates his ability to produce an impressive total effect by the use of detail. Every shot in this scene, and indeed in the whole of *The Legend of the Women's War*, introduces a new emotion vibrating between two extremes, rich comedy and lyrical gentle love. The comedy is introduced by Ctirad's escort, who cannot part with the jar of mead, and love is conveyed in this budding romance between Ctirad and Šárka. Šárka has been left as a bait with which to catch Ctirad. But though at the beginning she intends to deceive him, her own passionate feelings catch fire. It is in this scene that Trnka shows the gaiety with which he can handle the contradictions of love, a theme which he was to develop later in *A Midsummer Night's Dream*. He uses repeated sequences showing the knight in his grotesque attempts to get hold of the mead. His alcoholic dreams help

to underline the strong attraction between Ctirad and Šárka. The drunkard looks up and sees the couple in a strong embrace. Then again he is roused by the sound of a horn, and sees Ctirad with his head resting on Šárka's lap. The third time he comes to, it is only to gape at the ropes binding his legs.

The two men are taken prisoners by the women and taken to their castle. Then a more tragic motif begins. It is introduced by Vlasta. While she is harbouring ideas of revenge for the humiliation she suffered from Ctirad, the men set bonfires alight in celebration of the solstice. The rousing sound of a male chorus can be distinguished in the distance. The women listen sorrowfully, and in their mind's eye they picture a scene of feasting.

Meanwhile another group of men attack the castle. The forecourt thunders to the rhythm of dancing. Only Vlasta is determined to stand up to the men, arms in hand, to the very end. But one girl after another goes over to the other side. Vlasta remains alone with her rage. She prefers to go rather than to

Vlasta in *Old Czech Legends*

Amazons

Šárka

Ctirad and Šárka in *Old Czech
Legends*

Horymír
(scenario and
realisation)

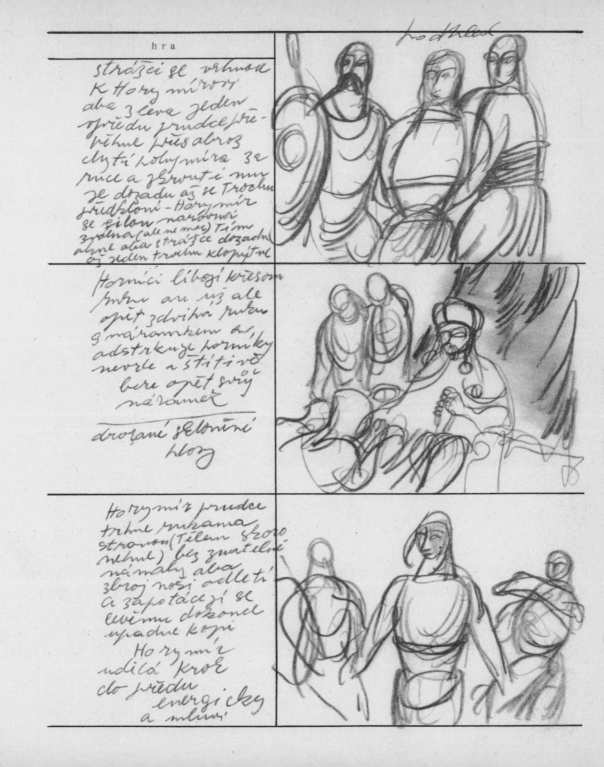

strážci se vrhnou
k Horymírovi
aby z leva jeden
zpředu prudce pře-
ruhne jiná abroz
chytí Horymíra ze
ruce a zkroutí mu
je dozadu až se trochu
předkloní – Horymír
se silou narovná
zpátky (ale ne moc) tím
ale ale strážce dozadu
až jeden trochu klopýtne

Hormíci líbají kresom
jednu au už ale
opět zdvihla ruku
s náramkem au,
odstrkuje hormíky
nevrle a štítivě
bere opět svůj
náramek

droçané şelonéné
hlory

Horymír prudce
trhne rukama
stranou (tělem skoro
nehnul) bez znatelné
námahy aba
zbroj noši odletí
a zapotácejí se
levému dokonce
upadne kopí
Horymír
udělá krok
do předu
energicky
a mluví

make her peace. Then the dance continues with renewed energy.

The next legend in the cycle, *The Legend of Křesomysl and Horymír*, is the weakest part of the film. Trnka failed to extract the full drama from the legend, and his interpretation has been criticised as mere story-telling.

He simply depicted the events of the story, without bringing any deeper insight to bear on it. He saw the theme simply as a moral tale about the evil influence of gold. These deficiencies, however, were due to a failure as a dramatist and script-writer. This part of the cycle was fully up to standard from the point of view of direction and design and, some of the scenes were very effective. The ancient mine which occurs in the story was most impressively designed, and the crowd scenes were admirably managed. Especially effective was the one where the angry gold miners react to the news that Horymír, leader of the opposing thanes, has complained about them to the prince. Another scene, which illustrated Horymír's prowess as a rider, outweighed all the shortcomings and suddenly lifted the interpretation to a much higher level. Trnka obviously found this scene most attractive, and included it because of its hidden possibilities. The movement of the horse, as it runs round the ramparts of Vyšehrad Castle, is filmed by a camera moving across the faces of the onlookers. The speed steadily increases. The faces almost merge into one another, and the beat of the hooves is accelerated to keep pace. Then comes the sudden leap up the battlements, a quick lift of the camera accompanied by the neighing of the horse, and the horse flies over the heads of the terrified goldminers ...

This showed Trnka's great art as a director. It was a unique example of arrangement, trick photography and animation, showing his masterly control of picture and sound.

The War Against the Lukanians falls somewhat outside the framework of the rest, and represents the climax of the work. It shows a rare unity of subject, form and style. In the preceding legends, with the exception of *The Legend of Bivoj*, Trnka tried to experiment with style. As the result the whole cycle has passages of uneven quality, lapses in dramatic effect and small obscurities in the story. *The War Against the Lukanians* was the sum of his experiments, in which everything was subordinated to a precisely defined idea of love for the homeland and its defence against attack from outsiders. It gives the whole cycle of *Old Czech Legends* a final depth of thought.

It opens with one puppet and a single word. In the empty hall of Vyšehrad Castle crouches the tiny lonely figure of Prince Neklan. He is addressed by a voice, impressive in its psychological impact. For a time it sounds like the voice of Neklan's conscience. Then it sounds from above, as though it is the voice of people in the beyond. Then the better and worse sides of Neklan seem to be conversing together. In whispers the voice encourages Neklan to be brave. Then with desperate insistence it paints the horrors caused by the Lukanians on the borders of the Czech lands. It describes with grotesque, ghostly pathos how the Lukanian General rose at midnight and growled like a wolf. Suddenly it sounds kind, as if talking to a child that needs gentleness and encouragement. In the end it grows in volume as it challenges Neklan to fight. The puppet tries to run away from it. He crouches at the wall and in corners, looks timidly around, hides his head in his hand, falls to the ground and runs away in an attempt not to hear anything.

Trnka found ideal interpreters for the scene in the voice of actor Karel Höger and in Břetislav Pojar who animated the puppet. Action and words merge to present a ful-blooded portrait of a human being. It is as though they lay bare his soul.

This scene is an introduction to the encounter between the Czechs and the Lukanians. Timorous Neklan hysterically refuses the weapon which is offered him. He has no strength to hold a sword in his trembling hand. So a youth of the people, Čestmír, takes the princes' harness and goes to the head of the host.

Darkness falls and the scene changes to the battlefield. Trnka depicts two identical scenes of grandeur, which are however sharply in contrast in character and atmosphere. Both armies stand poised for battle. The leaders address the warriors.

The first to speak is the leader of the Lukanians, Vlastislav. His address is curt. As an undertone, there is the sound of the growling of wolves and the screeching of birds of prey. Vlastislav takes up an arrogant pose, his dark red cloak fluttering in the breeze. On a leash he holds a creature which is half man and half beast. Vlastislav, as he addresses his men, is photographed from the front. The puppet's face fills the screen, and we merely feel the presence of the warriors round him. We do not see them; they appear only at the very end as the camera moves rapidly across them, a horde hungry for battle, flourishing their weapons. They remain nameless agents of the aggressive desires of their prince.

The scene in the Czech camp is quite different. It is almost lyrical. In the silence the twitter of birds can be heard, and a cuckoo calls in the distance. The warriors show that they have heard it. The paradox between the Czech superstition that a cuckoo foretells long life, and the fact that the soldiers are preparing for battle in which many of them

Neklan abandoned, in *Old Czech Legends*

will find death, creates a strong poetical feeling. Čestmír refers to it in his address:

'In vain,' he says, 'is thy call, cuckoo, in vain thou callest thy soothsay. It is not thine to choose a brief or long life for our people...'

There is a touch of melancholy about this introduction. During the speech the camera slowly moves over the assembled company as the warriors listen to their leader. Even Čestmír's gestures are slow and unemotional. In contrast to the other scene, the camera does not look into Čestmír's face as he delivers his speech. It shows him either from the side or from the back, and concentrates on the listening troops. The varying moods of his speech are reflected on their faces. The figures stand erect. Their posture and gestures reveal their determination and decision.

The change from the melancholy mood of the introduction to the mood of determined resistance is achieved in three shots, and one interrogative sentence:

'What is the use of my many springs, under the yoke of slavery, my enslavement and that of our women and children — all slaves?'

As these words are flung across the assembled troops they seem to add the power of thought to physical strength. 'And if there be death for me on the field of battle and ours be the victory ... oh, good will be

our fate. We shall live for ever in the songs of the old men, for the encouragement of men, women and children ... free people all.'

The emphasis on the last words is achieved by a grand panorama, filled with armed men, and Čestmír in the foreground raising his sword in a mighty gesture.

This is the culminating moment in the whole of *Old Czech Legends*. The audience receive only the impact, without knowing the restrained, precise composition, the various means by which the feeling is produced, by grading from shot to shot.

The actual battle scene begins with an attack by beasts and birds of prey. An effective background of sound augments the picture: the screeching of birds, the whistle of arrows as they are shot into the air, the howling of dogs. As the two armies engage in battle, a monotonous repetition of booming and voices underpaints the picture, vividly evoking the merciless machine of war.

In its technique, the battle is the most exacting sequence of the whole film. To control a picture full of figures in which each carried out a precise action, and to express the chaos of battle without allowing it all to turn into confusion was an immensely difficult task. Trnka decided to show the length of

Neklan's te

Sorrowing mother, in *Old Czech Legends*

the battle by a prolonged duel between Vlastislav and Čestmír. The red ball of the sun is sinking to the horizon before Česmír stands victor over Vlastislav. But he himself pays for his heroism with his life. He is surrounded and overpowered by a crowd of Lukanians. His heroic sacrifice stirs the faint-hearted Czechs, and they decide the battle in their favour.

The epilogue to *The War Against the Lukanians* forms the epilogue for the whole film. Over the body of the dead youth is a burial mound overgrown with grass. On the former battle-field corn is waving in the breeze. An old man with a lyre is walking through the cornfield. Choral singing is heard as he repeats Čestmír's words before the battle: 'Oh, good will be our fate. We shall live for ever in the songs of the old men . . .'

WITH *Old Czech Legend* Trnka won the day decisively. The conflicts which had arisen around *Bayaya* were forgotten. From lyricism, Trnka had turned to drama, and now to a mighty self-contained epic. He had developed his puppets until he could now depict an individual. The new style he had found was full of promise for the future.

Trnka's presentation of the legends was too contemporary not to run counter to the accepted image, taken from the classics. But the popular spirit and the patriotism with which it was imbued provided an answer to his opponents, and basically, there were no disputes as to its intention.

Experiments in puppet dialogue
The Two Frosts
The Schweik *series*
Acknowledgement to Josef Skupa
Whether puppetry had reached its limit

12

FOR SOME TIME now Trnka had been fascinated by the absorbing problem of introducing more dialogue into his puppet films. After his experiences when filming *Old Czech Legends*, to which this had added such a powerful effect, he could not resist the temptation to develop it further. He now realised that he needed to make his puppets speak in order to infuse new life into them. Prior to this film he had used words only with caution, as in *The Story of the Double-Bass* and *Bayaya*. In *Old Czech Legends* he used them in a much more complicated and exacting manner. A dignified monologue introduced in the form of an outside commentary had considerable impact, and in addition to this, the puppets themselves spoke several times.

This left Trnka only a small stage from expansion into more dialogue, with all the added attraction of fuller characterisation and entertaining repartee.

He now began to test the various possibilities of this and how he could best apply it to the medium of the puppet film.

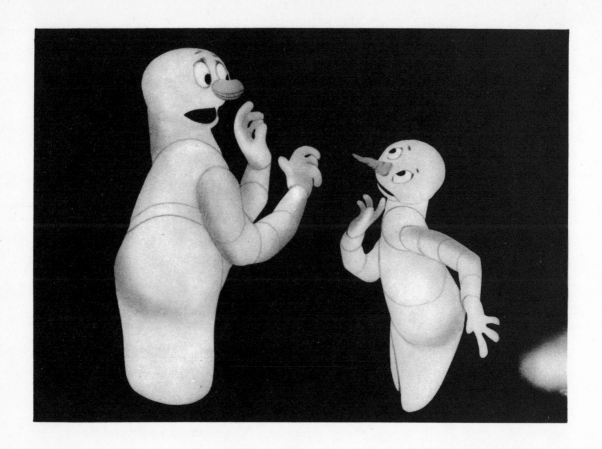

IN THE FAIRY TALE OF *The Two Frosts* he still temporised, lacking as yet the courage to let the puppets themselves speak the dialogue. These little three-dimensional figures therefore remained silent. Only the fairy-tale figures of the two Frosts, which were cut out of paper, spoke. Technically he found this simpler, for his many years of experience with animated cartoons had taught him how to use spoken words in conjunction with flat pictures. In this film the two paper figures were very near to drawn pictures while the puppets were quite a different proposition. From Walt Disney's

The Good Soldier Schweik

films Trnka had learnt that a stylised visual production needed corresponding stylisation in any accompanying voices used. With this in mind Trnka invited two comedians to work with him, who were sufficiently skilled as vocal caricaturists to deliver his dialogue in the exaggerated and bizarre manner necessary for his subject. The two actors he chose, both well known on the living stage, were Jan Werich, who spoke the part of the boastful old Frost, Bluenose, and Vlasta Burian, who spoke for the inexperienced Rednose, always ready to learn.

The main plot of the story was still acted in silent mime, but the scene introducing it was accompanied by speech. The two Frosts chase each other in a snow-covered landscape and discuss their talents for biting people. Two puppet heroes appear. The first is a rich peasant with a fur-lined coat, the second a poor little peasant with a coat only of cat-skin. The two Frosts cast lots for their prey, and this results in Bluenose taking on the poor peasant, and Rednose the rich one.

Next follows the part in silent mime. The boastful Bluenose is foiled in mishap after mishap. The poor little peasant proves to be a tough old man who circumvents all the Frost's tricks. He keeps himself warm in spite of them by walking briskly, cutting faggots, and getting together a good stock of fuel. Bluenose is completely defeated by his activities, gets trodden on himself, and has his back all bruised from the peasant's axe.

Rednose for all his inexperience is far more successful. His rich peasant is too lazy to move about to keep warm. He relies instead on his fur-coat to keep out the Frost's bites. Rednose makes quick work of freezing up his nose and ears, finally creeping right under his fur lining.

The final scene has dialogue again. It is evening on the village green. Rednose enters, satisfied with his day's work, after seeing the freezing peasant creep into bed. After a short interval Bluenose comes in looking worried and limping. At the sight of Rednose he determines to brazen out his defeat and starts boasting all over again. But the tough old peasant enters carrying a load of wood and Bluenose forgets what a brave hero he is pretending to be and runs away . . .

Although Trnka's use of words in *The Two Frosts* was really a kind of compromise it was nevertheless a genuine success. First-class design and the work of both an experienced puppeteer and animated cartoonist linked the two techniques of puppet play and paper figures to create the right atmosphere. The introduction of the right words spoken by two competent actors emphasised the bizarre nature of the story without detracting from the originality or poetic conception of the film as a whole.

The Two Frosts was really Trnka's first puppet film with dialogue successfully introduced. It maintained the standard he achieved in his three short films between *The Emperor's Nightingale* and *Bayaya*. Stimulated by the success of *The Two Frosts* Trnka launched himself on a larger project. This was the adaptation of J. Hašek's novel *The Good Soldier Schweik*.

HAŠEK'S NOVEL had more than two hundred characters drawn from all walks of life. These included middle class men and women, clerks, judges, policemen, stool pigeons, scientists, priests, ordinary Czechs, and the hierarchy of the Austrian officer class from the stupid non-com. to the Inspector-General. Through all these moved Schweik, a well-meaning fool, officially certified as mentally deficient. A man without the slightest intention of risking his neck for his Emperor.

This novel's wide success with the reading public and the interest centred in a character like Schweik had attracted many producers of both silent films and 'talkies', but they had all found adapting it full of problems. It was episodic. Each episode had certain characters in common, and each chapter its own dramatic theme. The character of Schweik was its main attraction, and every dénouement, whether sensible or ridiculous, was punctuated by his long reminiscences and anecdotes.

All these producers had worked roughly on the same system, cutting the story down to the wittiest scenes, which they strung together in a haphazard way. Their films were patchy, successful in parts but lifeless in others. This broke up the novel too much, conveying only glimpses of the vast world created by Hašek.

Trnka discarded this method of approach completely. Instead of selecting extracts he chose three complete chapters and made three separate films from them. The result was that his productions were more faithful to the original structure of the novel than those of his predecessors, and also he was able to make an original series of films, complete in themselves but with a common interest.

There is no doubt that it was Hašek's

humour which made Schweik so attractive a subject to Trnka in the first place. Then, also, Hašek's interpretation of the common man's hatred of war, in his brilliant satire of the Austrian war machine, was a theme with which Trnka had every sympathy. Also, above all else, Trnka was a puppeteer. Schweik, with his unmoved, never changing face, impenetrable, calm whatever was happening, and always victorious, had a real puppet's face. Now that Trnka had had success in introducing words into his puppet films he felt confident that they would strengthen his new creation.

THE FIRST of his set of three puppet films based on *The Good Soldier Schweik* is taken from chapter 3, volume 3: the story about the cognac which is considered to have the most literary merit. Hašek's text, read as a commetary by the actor Jan Werich, dominates the film, and even includes some dialogue. The story is then acted by the puppets as a complement to the text. By having the part that was read acted, and the part that was acted read, Trnka was attempting to keep his production predominantly literary. He was not entirely successful, as lack of co-ordination between the visual and the vocal presentations weakened the general effect.

Trnka based his designs for the film on Josef Lada's well-known illustrations to Hašek's books so that his characters had an appearance which had already been well popularised. He adapted this to suit his medium, where the caricature of every individual puppet had to be deliberate and to the point. This applied to the acting as well. Of all his puppet creations he excelled himself with the self-important fool Lieutenant Dub with his fatuous expression and his constant fussing about status.

Hašek's sub-plots, inserted into the main story, were included in the film in an effort to keep the full flavour of the novel. Trnka used a black and white paper technique for these, which were in strong contrast to the actual puppet scenes. The flat figures he used were divorced enough from reality to convey the exaggerated atmosphere of Schweik's stories, and in fact often turned them successfully into farce. On one hand they added charm of an original kind to the film, but on the other interrupted and weakened the main story. The transition from the black and white paper figures to the puppets was too mechanical, failing to evolve naturally, so that the film was broken up instead of being integrated. It was unfortunate that Trnka concentrated on being faithful to the structure of the novel. It meant that his first Schweik film suffered from being too literary in approach for its medium.

THIS SAME MISTAKEN approach also detracted from his second Schweik film, which was of the story of Schweik's accidents in the train. Again the individual sections cause the main thread to be lost. The spectator is constantly watching for something which never completely materialises. The acting, direction, and the words lack integration, dramatic impact is weakened, and the film is successful only in parts.

The different episodes were not connected by anything in common. Contrast is insufficient, and denouements not developed enough to stimulate interest. The spoken commentary was too vague and remote from the visual performance, and at one point the connection between them broke down altogether, though Trnka tried to gloss over this problem he had not solved as a joke. When the train goes through a tunnel the screen remains completely dark and empty, and the commentator's voice dominates alone.

However, in spite of its lack of unity, this film has its moments, particularly in one of the sub-plots where paper figures alternate with shadow figures.

The difficulties caused by the novel's original structure also tended to prevent the characters standing out as boldly as they would have done in a more straightforward story. Even so, many of Trnka's puppet characters were first-class caricatures, and the details of Schweik's adventures on the train reflect his talent, though the film as a whole is disjointed. As a whole the film reveals his lack of confidence in and dissatisfaction with his own line of approach.

HE NOW BROKE OFF his trilogy of Schweik films, interrupting it with quite a different kind of film, *The Circus Hurvínek*, in which he turned back to his teacher Josef Skupa's work. Skupa's well-known theatrical figures had been filmed before but only in documentaries on the theatre. When Trnka's animators started work on them it became obvious that he would have to re-create the two chief characters — Father and Son, as their heads, which were stylised for the theatre, were too unattractive in detailed close-ups. His new puppets, how-

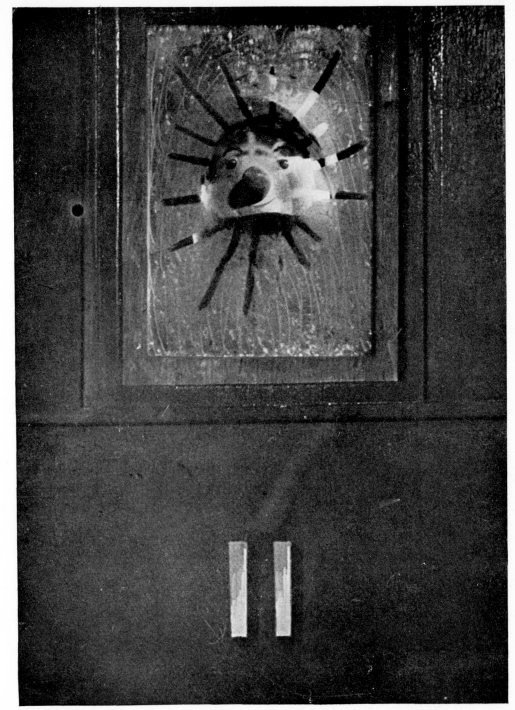

Schweik in the train

Circus Hurvínek

ever, kept Skupa's well-tested characteristics and their traditional dialogue. In both his Schweik films Trnka had used the text for the commentary. It was when filming *The Circus Hurvínek*, with a live dialogue, spoken by Skupa himself, that he realised how to solve the problems of his third Schweik film later on.

The Circus Hurvínek tells the story of two puppets, Daddy Spejbl and his son Hurvínek. Like most puppet plays it has a moral.

The boy puts on an act of being what he thinks is a good boy so that he will be given the money to go to the circus as a reward. He refuses to play football and pretends to be engrossed in his homework. Daddy Spejbl is mystified, and as he always lectures him whatever he is doing, now tries to persuade him to be naughty. Perpetual admonition is his idea of upbringing. But Hurvínek goes on pretending to be good for just as long as it takes him to get the money for the circus. The moment he has got this he starts being naughty all over again and slides down the banisters, landing head first. Then he falls asleep and has a horrible nightmare in which he is a lion-tamer whose animals won't do anything he tells them unless he lies and pretends to them all the time. He wakes up terrified and confesses that he has never really been a good boy at all but was only pretending he was.

Trnka faithfully followed the stage version, with its stress on the dialogue, as the two characters bicker incessantly. At least, this was his intention. But the film medium caused the dialogue to slip into second place as an accompaniment to the action and his two creations were weakened by this. The attraction of animated puppets is always different from the charm of marionnettes. Daddy Spejbl's marked characteristic movements, shrugging his shoulders and wagging his head, for example, were now able only to be suggested.

Yet although Trnka did not quite succeed in catching the full spirit of Skupa's theatre he did succeed in achieving his main object in making this particular film. This was to demonstrate his gratitude and respect to Skupa, his teacher. To Trnka himself as an artist this venture was to provide a lesson of permanent value, for through it he managed to solve the problems of puppet dialogue.

THIS PROGRESS WAS EVIDENT when Trnka followed *the Circus Hurvínek* with his third Schweik film. It is the reason why it is so much deeper and artistically more powerful than the two before. In these Schweik gives the impression of being a rogue and a wit. In this last film Trnka achieves a creation which conveys to the full Hašek's common man, never upset, destructive yet active, rebelling against those who have sent him to fight against his will and determined to lose every battle.

Trnka did not use a complete chapter from the novel for his third film. Instead he concentrated on Schweik's adventures with the gendarmes at the end of his pilgrimage.

The film has four main episodes, Schweik's arrest, his interrogation, his journey under escort to the town of Písek, and his return to the regiment. The height of drama is reached when the police officer suspects Schweik of being a Russian spy and treats him accordingly. By having far less commentary than before, introducing it only two or three times, Trnka allows the story to develop smoothly and naturally with the action. This lack of distraction and interruption allows individual characterisation to be stronger and more decisive than in the other two Schweik films. Jan Werich provided the voices for eight of the puppets, and his performance contributed greatly to the film's success.

The puppets themselves are so life-like that it seems quite natural for them to be talking. In fact, the spectator forgets that a human voice is speaking for them, and gets the impression that they are really doing it themselves. This is particularly convincing in the interrogation scene.

Three gendarmes, one of them an officer, are sitting on chairs facing Schweik. Every movement the officer makes is copied by the other two. Then he gets up and goose-steps to and fro, with his body stiff and erect. Each time he turns round by the wall he twists his head and looks at Schweik over his other shoulder, shooting questions at him all the time. It seems impossible to think of any actor capable of playing that scene so expressively, verging on caricature yet never wholly losing the individual character in the abstract idea of the officer. In his creation of Schweik, Trnka gave himself full play with facial expression. The puppet's face is no longer unmoved and impenetrable. Although the puppet in actual fact still has a fixed expression, Schweik now sits and smiles good naturedly. During the entire interrogation Schweik seems to be smiling contentedly as if he were enjoying himself, while his whole body is relaxed. From time to time he takes a pull at his pipe or scratches himself on the back.

Schweik's journey to Písek escorted by a gendarme makes another equally good scene. They both go pub crawling. The gendarme gets drunk and starts pondering about humanity. While he is holding forth he falls over in the snow, gets up and falls again repeatedly. Schweik tries to pull him up as he falls down again on the ice and crawls on all fours, but he slips down again still holding forth. Trnka has no mercy on his foolish puppet. He shows a cruelty to be found, perhaps, only in Chaplin's films. He throws him about on the ground, lets him get snow all over his neck and beard, stands him upright and then topples him over again and again. By this humiliation he expresses the inner poverty of soul of the poor loyal and dutiful gendarme. As the puppet falls there is heard the sound of ironic laughter mocking at human folly and depravity.

Paper figures are used twice in this film. The first time they illustrate one of Schweik's reminiscences, fortunately a short one, not long enough to interrupt the main story. The second time they rise up on a paper from which Schweik is drunkenly reading a report from Písek headquarters. In this context they are able to be slipped back naturally from the upright to the flat without disrupting the integration of the story.

TRNKA'S SCHWEIK, in spite of its imperfections, is still one of the best film creations based on Hašek's novel. It bears the unmistakable stamp of the author and at the same time that of Trnka. It was while making the Schweik films that Trnka was able to test out to the full every way in which speech could be used in puppet films. By the third he could perhaps be said to have exhausted all its possibilities.

For all three of the films the décor he created was both precise and realistic, conveying a modern, yet puppet-like world. This bore no resemblance to the dream fantasies with which he surrounded the fairy tales, myths or legends of his other films. This was a defined décor depicting an actual known real period and environment.

For Trnka, Schweik was then an experiment in design and material. It also constituted for him a climax to all his previous efforts at strongly individual characterisation.

The puppets themselves and their performance in *Old Czech Legends* were created with quite as much strength as those in the Schweik series. The difference between them lay in their nature, for being mythical and more remote they were less clear cut. For example Bivoj and Čestmír could both have the same performer. In a Schweik film, on the other hand, no puppet could act a dual interchangeable role. Schweik must be Schweik alone, Dub must be Dub, and none of the other puppet characters could act more than one part.

With the Schweik series Trnka had developed his pupet films to their uttermost. Another step and the puppet would have lost its *raison d'être*. It would have begun to displace the living actor.

Schweik's adventures
with the gendarmes

Schweik meets Lukas

Trnka's Revulsion from Puppets
State Prize
Recognition from Writers
Book Illustrations
Shakespeare and Trnka's Return to Puppets

13

MORE THAN eight years had passed since the day when Trnka left the studio where he had made his animated cartoons and began to use puppets for the first time, beginning with the crib scene which was to form the nucleus around which grew the first puppet film *The Czech Year*. Apart from a short period of hesitation, between *Bayaya* and *Old Czech Legends*, these eight years had

been devoted to mastering the techniques of the puppet film.

It was a long road between *The Czech Year* and *The Good Soldier Schweik*. Trnka had progressed from the moving doll to the puppet character, so alive that it could support the gift of speech.

During those eight years, Trnka made eleven puppet films, and one film with paper cut-outs. He also designed figures and décors for three films made by Břetislav Pojar. It was no exception for him to work a sixteen-hour day. Physically alone, this was exhausting. He wrote in the mornings, directed during the day, designed puppets and décors in the evening. This intensive creative work, with its tensions, the close concentration required, and the constant self-discipline, made the need for relaxation all the more urgent.

For a long time, Trnka suppressed this need. His natural liking for activity predominated. But he had felt a crisis impending when he had finished *Bayaya*, and it had been dispelled only when, after a brief escape from puppet films, he had started the exciting task of *Old Czech Legends*. He had suppressed the need for a longer rest while he struggled with this demanding script. But the moment he had finished *The Good Soldier Schweik*, and knew that he had reached another turning point, and must start all over again, then tiredness suddenly laid its claim.

The form it took was unexpected, and yet, in a way, logical. All his life Trnka had been looking for new ways to express himself with puppets. His book illustrations and free painting had merely been preparations for the puppet film. Now, after the success he had achieved with the puppets, he had a sudden reaction against them. He began to hate them, for he had the feeling that they were overpowering him, and had become a burden under which he would stumble if he did not get rid of it.

He had experienced a revulsion of this kind before, when, at the end of the war, he had wanted to run away from book illustration. But now he felt it with much greater intensity. He was forced to rebel against himself. And, as was to be expected, he abandoned the puppet film to seek refuge in illustrations.

EVERY TIME Trnka retraced his steps, he seemed, by some paradox, immediately to achieve recognition for his past work. Thus he reached his greatest fame as an illustrator when he was fully occupied with animated cartoons. Years later, he was acclaimed as 'the first rebel against Disney', when really he regarded animated films as a step towards puppet films, and was about to leave them behind. The same was true now. As he approached a crisis and left the studio for a while in order to illustrate books, he received the greatest acknowledgement he had yet known for the work he had already accomplished.

Trnka had achieved success internationally with *The Czech Year*, which was first shown at the 1948 Biennale in Venice, where it attracted considerable attention, and was awarded a Gold Medal. Those with foresight realised that *The Czech Year* had brought a new personality into the cinema, and that Trnka was a man with something to say and a unique way of saying it. His later films also won him international fame. *The Emperor's Nightingale*, *Bayaya* and *The Happy Circus*, all won prizes, while *Old Czech Legends*, *The Song of the Prairie* and *The Good Soldier Schweik* were highly praised.

But it was in 1954 that Trnka reaped his real success: in that year, just as he reached his point of crisis, he was awarded a State prize for pioneering work in puppet films. In 1955, the Government of the Republic bestowed the title of Distinguished Artist on him. These two years, and those which followed, were the period of real success, when his work was most fully understood and appreciated.

Not that Trnka ever did achieve complete comprehension from the critics, even though he gained public recognition. A poet himself, he was most truly understood and accepted by his fellow poets. To them his films were not merely marvels of technique: they were miracles of poetic expression. The most widely differing personalities responded to this aspect of his work. Each understood it in his own manner, but they all agreed on his greatness.

'I know two poets of the film,' said Nazim Hikmet, the Turkish poet. 'Charlie Chaplin and Jiří Trnka.'

'Trnka — the name is the sum of childhood and poetry,' wrote Jean Cocteau. 'He brings us back to a paradise from which the sad necessities of life have made us more and more remote. Trnka's films strengthen my opinion: the film as we know it is still far from being a developed art form. The cinema is a dead concept. Once people used to go to the cinema regardless of the value of the film they were seeing. But the true art of the film is still in its initial phases and is only beginning to win its spurs. The film in this sense is an original medium which gives limitless scope of expression. Trnka has shown this anew.'

Boris Polevoy, the well-known Soviet writer, had this to say:

'It may seem incredible, but I once spent a whole long day in the cinema. One film followed the other, almost without a break. There were works of the greatest variety: a comedy of life, sharp satire, merry and heroic fairy tales, and finally a truly poetic epic, imbued, as were all the works, with the wisdom and sublime simplicity of popular poetry. All the actors were puppets. But what puppets, and how they played!'

Quotations such as these could be made endlessly. Suffice it to conclude with the words of Pablo Neruda, the Chilean poet:

'Jiří Trnka does not yet occupy a place worthy of him. He is one of the contemporary world's greatest poets.'

The acknowledgement of the poets lent authority to Trnka's work, by emphasising the depth which had gone unnoticed. But, because it came at Trnka's period of crisis, it made him feel all the more that his work in puppet films was work accomplished. He felt detached from it now, as though this praise was for something he had parted with, and which now existed independently of him, having no bearing on his problems.

Under similar circumstances, a man of different temperament might have sought relief in a period of inactivity. Trnka, however, could not do without activity. This was not because he disciplined himself into doing a certain amount of work daily, or pushed himself by an exercise of will-power. It was

simply that work was a necessity to him, and he could not do without it. So he turned to illustrations again. Just as once the painter had suppressed the puppeteer, so, in later years, the puppeteer had obviously suppressed the painter. The hidden instinct to express himself in line and colour rose to the surface once again.

THE FIRST PERIOD of Trnka's concentrated interest in book illustration had ended in May 1945. After the liberation of Czechoslovakia, he had illustrated a book of twelve fairy tales, but he was already deeply involved in films. Although films had become his main interest, Trnka the illustrator had not been wholly suppressed. The books he had illustrated previously were reprinted, and his work in this field, far from being forgotten, continued to enhance his reputation. He did not, however, illustrate any new books. During those years he published three books with stand-up illustrations, but the drawings were taken from films on the same subjects.

During the pause after making *Bayaya*, when he made his short films, he had also returned to book illustrations, and with considerable success. He illustrated *The Thousand and One Nights*. This was not his first excursion into oriental subjects: one of his earlier illustrated books had been *Caravan*, which also had an oriental theme. But something had changed between the two. When Trnka did *The Thousand and One Nights* he was too engrossed in films for this not to show.

He used water-colours and fine pencil drawing, evoking the turbaned figures, the spirits, the jinn from the depth of his imagination as he always had. As before, he included black and white drawings, and made some full-page illustrations. But the artist's dream was more disciplined than it used to be: his treatment had gained in concentration. In *Caravan* there had been a loose arrangement of figures set in unreal space, but in *The Thousand and One Nights* Trnka set his figures more clearly in real space, and kept more closely to the traditional interpretations of the scenes. He tended to a decorative approach. For merit, it is difficult to choose between the two books, which have a decade between them. The illustrations to *Caravan* have a dream-like transient quality, while those in *The Thousand and One Nights* are slightly limited in their imaginative appeal by the close description of the setting. At the same time, Trnka had not lost his sense of

Deštník

poetry and his ability to make evocative associations, and his drawings in *The Thousand and One Nights* gave a strong impression of increased skill and maturity.

This book was the first high-light of Trnka's second period as an illustrator. It was published a few years after he had completed the drawings. The public had already encountered his illustrations in this second phase, for he had illustrated two books of poetry, Vítězslav Nezval's *Things,* *Flowers, Animals and People* and Jaroslav Seifert's *To Mother*. In both books he had evoked the world of his own childhood before the First World War: the world of oil lamps, sewing-machines, coffee grinders with brass handles, night-watchmen blowing on horns, and miraculous pocket watches.

But all these books had seemed just side-lines from Trnka's intensive work on films. It was in the autumn of 1954, when *The Good Soldier Schweik* was being completed,

Mlýnský kámen

that Trnka felt the need to break off work on films and concentrate on book illustration, and he signed several contracts with book publishing houses.

The illustrations he did during this time show him still experimenting. Though he had once been an innovator in the field of children's book illustration, progress had continued after he had left it for the films, and he now found the standard higher than it had been before. He could not pick up where he had left off. It still remained to find new mediums of expression, and to achieve the right balance between the demands of the text, the child reader, and his own imaginative conception. Trnka achieved varied success. Sometimes, it seems, the subjects were not entirely compatible with his own personal poetic vision.

Amongst the books he illustrated were fairy tales by František Hrubín, among them *Winter Fairy Tales*, some children's fables, a version of *Bayaya* and Hans Andersen's *Fairy Tales*. It was in the latter that his skill showed itself to the full. In this, his work was no longer experimental.

Trnka was fully in sympathy with the essential poetry of Hans Andersen, and he was able to capture its magical quality by a combination of his former ideas with his new maturity. He did not, as he had done in *Susan Discovers the World*, depart from the actual setting and situation, interpreting it in a composite picture. He drew the actual settings and situations, but in a way which expressed their underlying poetic emotion. His work was more decorative than it had been in his earlier books, but now the decoration did not lose itself in detail. It was not ornamental, it had an emotional function. He used full-page coloured illustrations, and small black and white drawings as chapter endings. Where he felt decoration would be intrusive, he used simple but impressive sketches. Some of his drawings, not surprisingly, show an affinity with scenes from his puppet film, *The Emperor's Nightingale*. It was no coincidence that the illustrations to that story should have been the culmination of his work on the book. They formed with the text a self-contained poem. Indeed, the whole book was a work of poetry.

TRNKA was engrossed in book illustration for almost two years. But, though he had turned his back on films and puppets, he had not ceased to think about the puppet film. He realised that with *The Good Soldier Schweik* he had exhausted the possibilities open to him with the techniques he had so far mastered. If he had continued along that avenue, he would have denied the puppet its independence, since it would have had no qualities different from those of a living actor. Again, he had to make a fresh beginning.

Several ideas occurred to him. First he considered his old idea of making a film of *Don Quixote*. Then, for a short while, he toyed with the idea of doing a one-act opera, Mozart's *Bastien and Bastienne*. He thought of using a children's choir and solos, and evolving a new form of puppet opera. But he never went on with this idea. He had spent too much time experimenting with voices, and he felt now that it would be better to make his puppets silent again, and let them express his ideas through mime.

Illustration for the book *Květuška and Her Garden* (English title, *Primrose and the Winter Witch*)

But there was another subject which he had thought about increasingly over the years, and it was one which would give him scope for using some of the trends evident in his illustrations. It would suit his particular stage of development, enabling him to express the sense of beauty his latest illustrations had revealed, and his new liking for decoration, and for variety of shapes and colours. It was a subject which held great promise.

Trnka decided to make a puppet film of *A Midsummer's Night's Dream*.

Shakespeare without words: Shakespeare without Shakespeare.

Trnka had proved many times that he could make a success of his most ambitious

N EDĚLE

projects. But this time it seemed that he was going too far. No sooner had the news of his plans appeared in the Press than people began to ask themselves if such a plan could be practicable. Was Trnka over-estimating his own powers, and those of his puppets?

Trnka was not interested in such questions: he had no time for doubt. As always, when once he had submerged himself in a piece of work, he was convinced of its success. He felt instinctively that scepticism was unfruitful, and only likely to weaken him at the outset. Hesitation only brought obstacles. For him, creation was not a matter of accidental inspiration, but of determination and hard work. In giving concrete form to his poetic vision he measured and measured again, five times, seven times, planning every detail. He has been called a poet, and with truth. But the basis of all art is craftsmanship, and

Trnka's craftsmanship is as solid and honest as that of a joiner or a blacksmith. This could not ensure the success of his future work, but it could ensure its basic solidity as an honest job of work. He wanted what he created to stand as firmly as a good table stands, without coming apart at the joints. The art critics compared his studio, with truth, to the workshop of one of the old painters, where the master directed the work of his apprentices, and where art was not divorced from other activities.

To bring the created work to life required more than craftsmanship: it was a creative task. To the uninitiated there might seem to be some sort of magic in this giving of soul to dead matter. But there was nothing magical about it, unless there was magic in the fantastically hard work with which Trnka and his fellow workers approached their task.

And this time the task was *A Midsummer Night's Dream:*

Shakespeare without words.

A Midsummer Night's Dream
New Techniques
Colour and the Wide Screen
Interpretation, Décor, and Characterisation
Passion *and* The Cybernetic Grandma
National Artist

14

THE RETURN to the studio did not prove as easy as Trnka had imagined, for his two years' absence had made themselves felt. While he had been preoccupied with book illustrations, his colleagues had learned to manage without their master. Most of them were now over thirty, and from their own point of view it was high time for them to begin if they wished to do independent work. Trnka had always relied on his team, and had not given enough thought to attracting and training new young members. He had forgotten that the years were passing and that his apprentices would feel the need to do work of their own, and start to make their own plans.

Also, there had been technical innovations during the past few years, among them wide screen projection. Trnka had often shown his scepticism on this subject, but all the same he could not resist testing the novelty. It was not only the technical possibilities that interested him: he had to consider the distribution and export possibilities of his films. He did not wish, however, to rely exclusively on the wide screen, and he therefore made his new film in two versions, one suitable for the normal size screen and the other specially adapted to the new wide screen.

New colour techniques were required for the latter. Trnka had always used Agfacolor, but with the growing width of the screen the edges appeared out of focus. Eastmancolor was more sensitive, and more precise and naturalistic than Agfacolor, though it had a different range of colours. It was good for showing the difference in different textures: wood remained wood, leather leather, and plush plush. But there was a danger that the colours would look vulgar and give the effect of a colour print. Trnka worked according to his experience with Agfacolor, and the result showed that Eastmancolor was more treacherous than he had realised. It showed much sharper contrasts, and required a different technique with lighting, and so on. This meant that several weeks' work by the whole team was worthless, and had to be started again. Many purely technical experiments had to be made which delayed the work and slowed it down in its initial stages. This upset work on the more creative side.

As a result, the film took over two years to complete.

Sketch for *A Midsummer Night's Dream*

AFTER THE FIRST performance of *A Midsummer Night's Dream* the critics at home and abroad were surprised at what appeared to be an entirely new departure for Trnka: they could not see that the film had any logical place in his development. Some even asserted that he had been tempted by the subject merely to create a spectacle for the wide screen. This was not true, but it is true that, on the surface, the film seems to

18 colour stills from *A Midsummer Night's Dream*

fall outside the line he had been pursuing in puppet films.

In *The Czech Year* and *The Emperor's Nightingale* Trnka had made a beginning, using a primitive form of movement that was mainly symbolic. With *Bayaya* there had come a dividing line between symbolism and individual characterisation. Progress towards *The Good Soldier Schweik* had been in a straight line.

In *Schweik* the puppets had become increasingly individualised and capable of nuances of expression. The words had become organically linked with the acting of the puppets. Up to that point everything had been logical. Now it seemed that Trnka had thrown all his previous experience overboard. He had transposed Shakespeare's comedy into a fairy ballet. Words had receded again to an occasional commentary, its purpose

solely to elucidate the more complicated parts of the plot so that the spectator could follow them. Trojan's music had returned to the rôle it had played in Trnka's first films.

Yet, all the same, *A Midsummer Night's Dream* was organically part of Trnka's work as a whole, and its roots went deep. He had been preparing for it throughout all his preceding work. In *The Animals and the Brigands*

there can be traced the pattern of the dance of the elves, acorns and pine cones in the Athenian forest. In *The Czech Year* we find peasants and craftsmen: prototypes of Bottom the Weaver and his friends. In *The*

Story of the Double-Bass an incongruous nocturnal encounter, brought about through the agency of fate, is ironically depicted. In *The Women's War*, in *Old Czech Legends* Trnka deals satirically with the strange

ways of love, and the lovers' ecstasies that make fools of the wise.

In *A Midsummer Night's Dream* all these and many other elements are brought to fuller development. It was, moreover, typical of Trnka to take a subject and make it his own. He did this with *The Emperor's Nightingale*, with *Bayaya*, and with *Old Czech Legends*. Thus *A Midsummer Night's Dream* was something more than an adapta-

tion. It was an original variation on the theme, as original, for instance, as Prokofiev's ballet of *Romeo and Juliet*.

'A BALLET OF MIME and fairies': this was Trnka's own description of *A Midsummer Night's Dream*. It sums up its original quality: Shakespeare's comedy had found an interpreter of new dimensions. What

Shakespeare had achieved in words, Trnka interpreted in movement and artistic design. The balletic method was not wholly new to him: he had used it in some parts of *Old Czech Legends* but it had not, as now, been a basic element interpreting the theme. Trnka, in fact, had not returned to his earlier techniques, but had developed a new one from his past experience. In *The Emperor's Nightingale* the puppets were

silent, rather as actors were silent in the days before 'talkies'. But in *A Midsummer Night's Dream* the puppets were silent in the way that actors in mime, or ballet dancers, are silent. There was a basic difference in expression: in the first, the movement was symbolic, in the second, the action was expressed through the language of mime.

Mime is considered the most difficult form of acting, combining as it does some of the

features of both the dance and the drama. Its aim is to arouse tears or laughter in the audience without words. The demands on a living actor are heavy: in considering the obstacles facing Trnka and his assistants, we have to remember that his actors were not living. He was assisted by new materials from which to make his puppets: they were no longer of wood, but of plastic. Even so, it needed all his gifts of creative imagina-

tion, and all his technical skill in animation.

His reason for choosing this particular method of expression arose naturally from the act of transposing the atmosphere of Shakespare's comedy into a puppet film. He wanted to retain all the sparkle and lightness of the original, which he felt might have been lost by words delivered by puppet actors. He felt the fragile artistry could be preserved by a puppet ballet, which could

also interpret the three incongruous and incompatible worlds which collide in Shakespeare's play, and are forced by the magic of his imagination to play out a plot full of changes, tricks and unexpected twists.

Trnka's interpretation of these three worlds was a measure of his skill. Where Shakespeare had differentiated between them with words, Trnka used artistic designs of differing colours and shapes, and contrasting anima-

tion in his puppets. Each of the three worlds had its own character and atmosphere, its philosophy and manner, and each struck a different chord in the spectator.

First was the world of Theseus, Duke of Athens: one of smooth courtesy and obedience to traditional rules. In characterising this ostentatious environment, Trnka did not hesitate to link Antique, Renaissance and Rococo styles, to give the impression of cold and exaggerated culture, snobbery and formality. His approach is ironic: he uses slow, serious movements in animating the puppets, with a touch of parody. Theseus is depicted as a conceited old roué who always takes up an exalted pose, to show how much he stands on ceremony. Hippolyta, his Queen, the Queen of the Amazons, has a touch of barbaric beauty.

The four lovers also belong to this world. Demetrius, the soldier, is shown as a lumbering fellow, who is always stamping about as though he is on parade. He sees himself in the Duke to such an extent that he even tries to look like him, by copying the cut of his beard. Lysander, on the other hand, is a well-groomed blond with a flute and a rose, who dances as he walks.

Helena and Hermia are remarkable creations, who owe much to Trnka's earlier character, Šárka, in *Old Czech Legends*. It is almost unbelievable that puppets can convey so much of a young girl's charm. The two figures are remarkably expressive of budding womanhood and hidden coquetry, with their wide set eyes, full of secrets and a touching gentleness, while seeming at the same time to burn with the promptings of desire.

Trnka conveys nuances within the different worlds, as Shakespeare does, making the love *pastorale*, which is expressed in smooth verse by Shakespeare, different in atmosphere from the court, but having more in common with it than with the world of Bottom and his friends, conveyed by Shakespeare in pithy speech.

It is here, among the artisans, that Trnka shows himself most at home. His style is

Bottom (sketch and puppet)

A Midsummer Night's Dream;
Oberon

restrained, simple, poetical. Shakespearean scholars claim that Shakespeare's models were 'the old country craftsmen of the guilds and the apprentices he had known in his native Stratford'. Trnka drew on the characters he had known in Plzeň, even lending Bottom a little of his own personality. For was he not a fellow whose theatrical ambitions caused one upset after another? Had not Trnka himself once uttered that ridiculous and yet magnificent wish: 'Let me play the Lion, too'?

However that may be, the group of craftsmen undoubtedly provide the most artistically pure scenes in Trnka's *A Midsummer Night's Dream*. As soon as these six enthusiasts appear on the screen the comedy takes on a truly popular character. This is a world of noisy earthiness: a little clumsy, a little ridiculous, but strong in its enthusiasm for creation. When they begin to play their 'most lamentable comedy and most cruel death of Pyramus and Thisbe', when the moon begins to shine and the lion roars, and Bottom takes a step forward to assume his most tragic posture, Trnka achieves a

247

poetic strength that is to be found nowhere else in his work.

Bottom is the clue to Trnka's version of *A Midsummer Night's Dream*. That ardent artisan who, in every situation, knows a way out, and who is so enthusiastic about the theatre that he wants to play not only Pyramus and Thisbe, but also the lion, is not a purely comic character in Trnka's version. He has much in common with Schweik, not so much in design and animation as in personality. There is a trace of 'Schweikism' in the way Bottom lets himself be spoilt by the refined fairy attentions of Titania. And Bottom has something of Schweik about him when he appears before Theseus. Bottom is ridiculous, but beneath this exterior are concealed some lovable qualities, among them his diligence and his urge to create.

Having conceived him in this way, Trnka was able to bestow on Bottom a scene which does not appear in Shakespeare, but which was the most beautiful in Trnka's *A Midsummer Night's Dream*. The amateur actor suddenly turns into a real tragedian as he acts Pyramus' sorrow over the death of Thisbe. For a moment the comedy turns into tragedy, revealing hidden depths in him. Trnka made Puck responsible for this, in order to justify the change of his pattern. But Bottom is throughout an essentially creative character.

It is Bottom and Puck who unite the three incongruous worlds. These two characters must have been Shakespeare's favourites, and they were certainly Trnka's. He depicted them with no trace of the vulgarity which, in some productions, turns Bottom into a clumsy fool and Puck into a sexless creature. Trnka's fairy world was the world of natural dreams, which can influence even the fate of men. His Puck was not confused himself, but delighted in the confusion he caused to everyone else, to amuse himself. He is shown as an entirely purposeful rogue. Like any boy, when he has the magic flower in his hand, he has to try it out to see what it can do, leaving neither statues nor snails in peace, let alone human beings. He smiles at folly and conceit, making fun of the ostentation of his master, Oberon, who, blinded by his love for Titania, cannot decide whether to appear in front of her in clothes of fur, fruit or icicles. Puck is in his element when Demeter and Lysander start fighting. He is the moving force behind the comedy, the whole wood ringing with his doings.

In depicting the fairy world, Trnka allowed his imagination to roam, liberal in gifts, of beauty and spectacle. In the fairy wood, where

Oberon quarrels with Titania, ideas spurt and explode like fireworks. The seeds and insects come to life, the acorns dance with the mosses, the pine-cones and petals change into little imps. Oberon and Puck undergo constant changes, and Titania is so fragile that she floats on air, borne on a cloak woven by the fairies, beetles and glow-worms. Everything sparkles with magic, and yet it is all really disciplined and controlled. Had he taken one tiny turn in the wrong direction, the whole would have been a fiasco.

The whole film was animated with consummate skill. There were high-spots, among them Bottom's famous moment as Pyramus, his love scenes with Titania, Lysander serenading under Hermia's window, and so on, but these stand out only because of the extra scope they gave. There was no unevenness in the animation: it was of a high standard of excellence.

Trnka, as we know, had always looked with a critical eye at the idea of the wide screen. But having once decided to use it, he characteristically made the most of it. The subject of *A Midsummer Night's Dream* was eminently suitable. The outdoor scenes lent themselves exquisitely to being rendered in breadth. But Trnka was not content to accept any limitations the new screen might have imposed. If the situation demanded concentration, he did not hesitate to limit the scene to a section of the whole surface. He was not afraid to put two or three parallel events side by side, in the manner of a diptych or triptych, to heighten the effect. Thus he overcame many of the drawbacks imposed by the new screen, while at the same time discovering several new possibilities. It could even be said that he discovered the elements of using the new screen artistically, giving others a start. From that point of view, *A Midsummer Night's Dream* was an important work.

WHEN *A Midsummer Night's Dream* was shown at the Cannes Film Festival, it aroused immediate controversy. This was nothing new to Trnka: all his films had done so. But none had brought forth so many contrasting opinions.

'It is a film full of invention, humour, refinement, and we are fascinated by its rare beauty,' wrote the film critic of *Le Parisien Libéré*, full of enthusiasm.

'It is a fantasy of good taste and choreographic ideas, but deliberately over-refined,' said his colleague of the Milan *L'Unità*, coldly.

'Trnka sent even garden gnomes into

Shakespeare's realm,' said the correspondent of the *Stuttgarter Zeitung*, unkindly.

In Trnka's own country, where it was shown at People's Film Festivals, the film was better understood by the critics than any of his previous films had been. They discussed such questions as whether or not it was more poetic than *The Emperor's Nightingale*, less artistic than *The Czech Year*, more full of meaning than *The Good Soldier Schweik*. Meanwhile, at discussions following each performance, and in dozens of letters to Trnka personally, the audiences expressed their gratitude for a beautiful experience. With *A Midsummer Night's Dream* Trnka had won his most difficult battle: the battle for the appreciation of the public.

After the completion of *A Midsummer Night's Dream*, Trnka went back to book illustration-verse, fairy tales and Jirásek's *Legends of Old Bohemia*. He did work for an exhibition held in honour of the fifteenth anniversary of the Czechoslovak Republic. He made a gigantic map for the Czechoslovak Exhibition in Moscow.

He was away from the studio for three years, and it was three years during which, all over the world, animated films made the equivalent of ten years' progress. New centres were set up; new schools and new styles arose. Trick photography developed widely. It is no exaggeration to say that Trnka was responsible for all this. It was he who had rediscovered trick photography, and given it a new importance. He had shown that there was scope in animated cartoons and puppet films not only for originality, but for serious artistic expression.

Now, after three years, he found a new situation. He was faced with what others had achieved through following his example. He found that puppet films were growing stagnant in the face of growing competition from animated films.

The outcome of all this pressure was a film called *Passion*. This was a short film, but an important one for the development of puppet films. It was a grotesque morality play on the very topical subject of speed. Trnka set out to ridicule the passion of young men who think that the moment they own a motor bike they become lords of creation. He showed the life of one of these fanatics from birth to death, all compressed into a few moments. The film achieved something for which his disciples had been struggling vainly in his absence. It expressed an opinion on a contemporary subject by means of grotesque associations in design, by novel ideas full of impact, and by its compression

Figures in *Passion*

From *The Cybernetic Grandma*

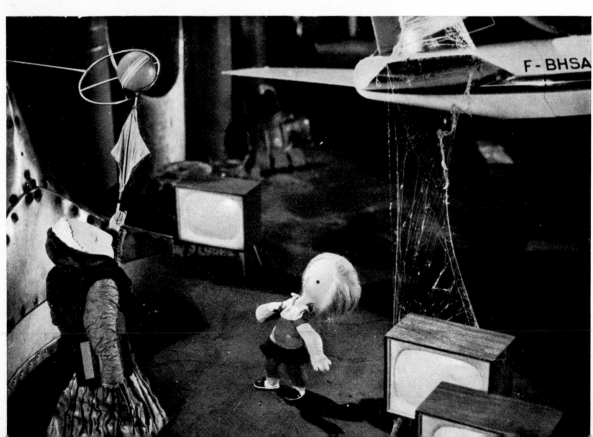

and economy. In it he evolved a new style. At the same time, it brought the puppet film close to the animated cartoon. It was an experiment in broadening the puppet film by using the potentialities of the animated cartoon, while retaining the specific qualities of the puppet film. It was a preparation for his next film, *The Cybernetic Grandma*. As with all his work, a short *étude* preceded a more significant piece of work.

The Cybernetic Grandma was an excursion into science fiction, and it was Trnka's most widely debated film of all. It was a work of bitter satire, full of deep feeling. In it, Trnka attacked the fetish of technology: man's enslavement by machines. He was not against technology and technical progress, but he was against the abuse of them, and their dehumanising influence.

He used a story by a young writer, Ivan Klíma, about a child and two grandmothers. One is a normal human grannie, with an umbrella and a camera, and the other, the cybernetic grandma, is a terrible, fantastic child-minding machine. The little girl lives on the old Earth with her human grannie while her parents are working on some planet. Then the parents, having been given somewhere to live, want their child to join them. She is entrusted to an automatic device which transports her with scientific precision to her destination. In the absence of her parents, a cybernetic grandma is to look after her at home. This is a large moving chair with an electric eye that can tell stories, throw a ball, play hide-and-seek, do exercises, and even teach the child. But the game turns into a chase of terror, with the machine stampeding. It tries to lure the child with sweet words, and chases her hysterically round the empty flat. The plot is an excuse for a confrontation between the two grannies.

The basic idea, man and his relationship to the machine, was not a new one for Trnka. He had handled it first in *The Emperor's Nightingale*. There, too, the child had been overpowered by the empty mechanical guardian blindly apportioning his time, and there, too, the machine and living being had confronted each other. But in *The Emperor's Nightingale* the warning was buried in the magic of the fairy tale. Here it was presented more harshly and with far greater insistence, just as the need for such a warning had become more urgent during the thirteen years between the two films.

Thus, just as Trnka had spoken to his contemporaries by evoking the past in *Old Czech Legends*, so he again addressed the present generation by evoking the future in *The Cybernetic Grandma*. It is this artistic relevance which gives Trnka's work its lasting virtues, and which shows too its organic development from traditional forms.

The Cybernetic Grandma is Trnka's latest film to date. His work still continues. He remains active as an illustrator, and is still on the look-out for new themes for his films.

On July 30th, 1963, Trnka was given the title of National Artist, a rare distinction, and a well deserved recognition of his oeuvre to date.

BOOKS ILLUSTRATED BY JIŘÍ TRNKA

Author - Original Title	English Title	Original Publication		English Publication
Vítězslav Šmejc: Tygr pana Boška	Mr. Boška's Tiger	*Šolc a Šimáček*	*1937*	
Vítězslav Šmejc: Tygr jede k moři	The Tiger at the Seaside	*Šolc a Šimáček*	*1937*	
Josef Menzel: Míša Kulička v rodném lese	Bruin Furryball in his Forest Home	*Melantrich*	*1939*	*Dakers, 1957*
K. Andersen: Ve spárech oceánu	In the Claws of the Ocean	*Melantrich*	*1939*	
Josef Menzel: Míša Kulička v cirkuse	Bruin Furryball in the Circus	*Melantrich*	*1940*	*Dakers, 1957*
K. J. Erben: Pohádky	Fairy Tales	*Melantrich*	*1940*	
Helena Chvojková: Zuzanka objevuje svět	Susan Discovers the World	*Melantrich*	*1940*	
Jan Karafiát: Broučci	The Fireflies	*J. Otto*	*1940*	

Author - Original Title	English Title	Original Publication		English Publication
Kuzma:				
Vilém Tell	William Tell	*Unie*	*1940*	
J. Hudec:		*Dědictví*		
Slovenské národní pohádky	Slovak Folk Tales	*Komenského*	*1940*	
Josef Menzel:				
Míša Kulička v zoo	Bruin Furryball in the Zoo	*Melantrich*	*1941*	*Dakers, 1957*
J. Glazarová:				
Advent	Advent	*Melantrich*	*1941*	
Wilhelm Hauff:				
Karavana	Caravan (Fairy Tales)	*Melantrich*	*1941*	*Paul Hamlyn, 1961*
R. Billinger:				
Čaronoc	Magic Night	*Melantrich*	*1941*	
J. Š. Kubín:				
V čarodějném kole	In the Magic Circle	*J. Otto*	*1941*	
J. V. Rais:				
Zvířátka a lidé	Animals and People	*Novina*	*1941*	
Captain Marryat:				
Kormidelník Vlnovský	Masterman Ready	*Melantrich*	*1942*	
Helena Rodlová:				
Strýc Jakub a Petříček	Uncle Jacob and Little Peter	*J. Otto*	*1942*	
The Brothers Grimm:				
Pohádky a legendy	Fairy Tales	*J. R. Vilímek*	*1942*	*Paul Hamlyn, 1961*
The Brothers Grimm:				
Děti Pána Boha	Children of God	*J. R. Vilímek*	*1942*	
Rudolf Slawitschek: Anastasius	Anastasius	*J. R. Vilímek*	*1942*	
Kočkodan, velký kouzelník	the Great Magician			
V. Renč:				
Marnotratný syn	The Prodigal Son	*Vyšehrad*	*1942*	

Author - Original Title	English Title	Original Publication	English Publication
František Hrubín:			
Říkejte si se mnou	Say It with Me	*Melantrich*	*1943*
V. K. Klicpera:			
Zlý jelen	The Naughty Deer	*Unie*	*1943*
K. Hlávka:			
Kormorán	Cormorant	*Vilém Šmidt*	*1943*
K. Hlávka:			
Benátská maškaráda	Venetian Masquerade	*Švejda*	*1943*
Jiří Horák:			
České pohádky	Czech Fairy Tales	*J. R. Vilímek*	*1944*
František Hrubín:			
Říkejte si pohádky	Tell a Fairy Story	*Melantrich*	*1946*
František Křelina:			
Zmijí dědek	Grandfather Viper	*Kolo mor. spis.*	*1946*
Jan Drda:			
Hrátky s čertem	Play with the Devil	*A. Hynek*	*1946*
Jiří Mahen:			
Dvanáct pohádek	Twelve Fairy Stories	*Družstevní práce*	*1947*
František Hrubín:			
Zasadil dědek řepu (leporelo)	Grandpa Planted a Beet	*ČSFN*	*1947*
František Hrubín:			
Zvířátka a petrovští (leporelo)	The Animals and the Brigands	*ČSFN*	*1948*
Vítězslav Nezval:			
Věci, květiny, zvířátka a lidé (pro děti)	Things, Flowers, Animals and People	*Čs. spisovatel*	*1953*
Jan Páleníček:			
České pohádky	Czech Fairy Stories	*SNKLHU*	*1953*

Author - Original Title	English Title	Original Publication		English Publication

Jaroslav Seifert:

Maminka	To Mother	*Čs. spisovatel*	*1954*	

Jan Alda:

Jak stařeček měnil (leporelo)	How Grandpa Changed till Nothing was Left	*SNDK*	*1955*	

František Hrubín:

Pohádka o Květušce a její zahrádce	Primrose and the Winter Witch (retold by James Reeves)	*SNDK*	*1955*	*Paul Hamlyn, 1964*

Vladimír Holan:

Bajaja	Bayaya	*Čs. spisovatel*	*1955*	

František Hrubín:

Zimní pohádka o Smolíčkovi	A Winter's Tale	*SNDK*	*1955*	

Oldřich Syrovátka:

Bajky dětem	Legends for Children	*SNDK*	*1955*	

Hans Christian Andersen:

Pohádky	Fairy Tales	*SNDK*	*1955*	*Paul Hamlyn, 1959*

J. K. Tyl:

Strakonický dudák	The Strakonice Bagpiper	*SNKLHU*	*1956*	

Josef Menzel:

Mischa Kugelrund im Puppentheater	Bruin Furryball in the Puppet Theatre	*Artia*	*1956*	*Dakers, 1957*

Josef Menzel:

Mischa Kugelrund im Spielzeugsparadies	Bruin Furryball in the Toyhouse	*Artia*	*1956*	*Dakers, 1958*

František Hrubín:

Špalíček pohádek	A Tree of Fairy Stories	*Čs. spisovatel*	*1957*	

František Hrubín:

Dvakrát sedm pohádek	Twice Seven Fairy Stories	*Čs. spisovatel*	*1957*	

Author - Original Title	English Title	Original Publication		English Publication
František Hrubín:				
Dvě veselé pohádky	Two Merry Stories	*Čs. spisovatel*	*1957*	
František Hrubín:				
Pohádky tisíce a jedné noci	Tales from the Arabian Nights	*Čs. spisovatel*	*1957*	*Paul Hamlyn, 1960*
Vítězslav Nezval:				
Zlatý věk	The Golden Age	*SNDK*	*1957*	
Charles Perrault:				
Pohádky	Fairy Stories	*SNKLHU*	*1959*	
William Shakespeare:				
	A Midsummer Night's Dream	*Artia*	*1960*	
Eduard Petiška (retold for children):	A Midsummer Night's Dream	*Artia*	*1960*	
A. Jirásek:				
Staré pověsti české	Legends of Old Bohemia	*SNDK*	*1960*	*Paul Hamlyn, 1963*
Jiří Trnka:				*Golden Pleasure*
Zahrada	Through the Magic Gate	*SNDK*	*1962*	*Books, 1963*
Jean de La Fontaine:				*Golden Pleasure*
Bajky dětem	Fables	*SNDK*	*1961*	*Books, 1963*

FILMS BY JIŘÍ TRNKA

S - Subject; Sc. - Scenario; D - Directed; A - Art Director; C - Collaborated; ct. - cut; Cm - Commentary

Original Title		English Title	Type of Film	Trnka's Participation
Zasadil dědek řepu	1945	Grandpa Planted a Beet	*Animated Cartoon*	*S, D, A*
Dárek	1946	The Gift	*Animated Cartoon*	*S, Sc., D*
Pérák a SS	1946	The Chimney Sweep	*Animated Cartoon*	*Sc., D, A*
Zvířátka a petrovští	1946	The Animals and the Brigands	*Animated Cartoon*	*Sc., D, A*
Liška a džbán	1947	The Fox and the Jug	*Animated Cartoon*	*A*
Špalíček	1947	The Czech Year	*Puppet Film*	*S, Sc., D, A, ct.*
Císařův slavík	1948	The Emperor's Nightingale	*Puppet Film*	*Sc., D, C, A, ct.*
Árie prérie	1949	The Song of the Prairie	*Puppet Film*	*D, Sc., C, A*
Román s basou	1949	The Story of the Double–Bass	*Puppet Film*	*Sc., D, A*
Bajaja	1950	Bayaya	*Puppet Film*	*D, Sc., C, A*
Čertův mlýn	1951	The Devil's Mill	*Puppet Film*	*Sc., D, A*
O zlaté rybce	1951	The Golden Fish	*Animated Cartoon*	*Sc., D, A*
Perníková chaloupka	1951	The Gingerbread Cottage	*Puppet Film*	*A*
Veselý cirkus	1951	The Happy Circus	*Paper cut-outs*	*Sc., D, A, C*
Jak stařeček měnil až vyměnil	1952	How Grandpa Changed till Nothing was Left	*Animated Cartoon*	*D, A*
Kuťásek a Kutilka	1952	Kuťásek and Kutilka	*Puppet Film*	*Sc., D, C*
Staré pověsti české	1953	Old Czech Legends	*Puppet Film*	*Sc., C, D, A*

Original Title		English Title	Type of Film	Trnka's Participation
Dva mrazíci	1954	The Two Frosts	*Animated Cartoon*	*Sc., D, A*
O skleničku víc	1954	A Drop Too Much	*Puppet Film*	*A*
Osudy dobrého vojáka Švejka	1954	The Good Soldier Schweik	*Puppet Film*	*Sc., D, A*
Byl jednou jeden král	1955	There Was Once a King	*Film with living actors*	*A*
Cirkus Hurvínek	1955	Circus Hurvínek	*Puppet Film*	*Sc., C, D, A*
Jan Hus	1955	The Hussite Warrior	*Film with living actors*	*A, C*
Spejbl na stopě	1955	Spejbl on the Track	*Puppet Film*	*A*
Jan Žižka	1956	Jan Žižka	*Film with living actors*	*AC*
Proti všem	1956	Against All	*Film with living actors*	*AC*
Paraplíčko	1957	The Little Umbrella	*Puppet Film*	*AC*
Sen noci svatojánské	1959	A Midsummer Night's Dream	*Puppet Film*	*Sc., C, D, A, Cm*
Vášeň	1962	Passion	*Puppet Film*	*S, Sc., D, A*
Kybernetická babička	1963	The Cybernetic Grandma	*Puppet Film*	*Sc., D, A*

A Midsummer Night's Dream (lithograph)

PRIZES AND AWARDS

1946   INTERNATIONAL FILM FESTIVAL, CANNES: Prize for the film *The Animals and the Brigands*
Prize of Bohemia for the film *The Animals and the Brigands*

1947   Prize of the Czechoslovak Film Critics for the film *The Czech Year*
VENICE BIENNALE: Prize for the film *The Village Feast* (from *The Czech Year*)
BRUSSELS: Honourable Mention for the film *Bethlehem* (from *The Czech Year*)

1948   VENICE BIENNALE: Gold Medal for the film *The Czech Year*
PARIS: Prix Méliès for the film *The Legend of St. Procopius* (from *The Czech Year*)

1949   Czechoslovak National Film Prize for the film *The Emperor's Nightingale*
PARIS: International Film Festival of Cartoons and Puppet Films: First prize for *Pilgrimage* (from *The Czech Year*)

1950   Czechoslovak National Film Prize for the film *Bayaya*
INTERNATIONAL FILM FESTIVAL, KARLOVY VARY: First Prize in the puppet films class for *Bayaya*
PARIS: Prix Méliès for the film *The Emperor's Nightingale*

1951   INTERNATIONAL FILM FESTIVAL, EDINBURGH: Honourable Mention for the film *The Song of the Prairie*
PARIS: Prix de la critique for the film *The Emperor's Nightingale*

1952   PARIS: Prix Méliès for the film *The Song of the Prairie* and second prize for *The Happy Circus*
INTERNATIONAL FILM FESTIVAL, EDINBURGH: Honourable Mention for the film *The Happy Circus*
INDIA: Honourable Mention for the film *The Song of the Prairie*

1953   VENICE BIENNALE: Silver Medal and Special Award from the President of the Biennale for the film *Old Czech Legends*
Honourable Mention in the short films for young people class for the film *Bivoj* (from *Old Czech Legends*)
INTERNATIONAL FILM FESTIVAL, LOCARNO: Prize of the Swiss Film Critics for the film *Old Czech Legends*

1954   Czechoslovak State Prize Winner
INTERNATIONAL FILM FESTIVAL, LOCARNO: Grand Prix of the Swiss Film Critics for the film *Bayaya*

INTERNATIONAL FILM FESTIVAL, KARLOVY VARY: Czechoslovak Prize in the puppet films class for *The Good Soldier Schweik*

ALGERIA: Prize of the Association of Cultural Organisations for the best film of the year to *Bayaya*

MONTEVIDEO FILM FESTIVAL: Grand Prix in the puppet films class for the film *Old Czech Legend*

BELGIUM: Second Prize in the enquête of the Belgian Ciné-club Écran du séminaire for the film *The Song of the Prairie*

1955   Awarded the Czechoslovak Honour: Merited Artist

WARSAW FILM FESTIVAL: Grand Prix (hors concours) for the film *Old Czech Legends*

BRITISH FILM ACADEMY: Prize for the film *The Song of the Prairie*

AMERICAN FILM ACADEMY: Golden Reel for the film *The Emperor's Nightingale*

1956   MONTEVIDEO FILM FESTIVAL: Grand Prix for the film *The Good Soldier Schweik*

OBERHAUSEN: Week of Cultural Films: Prize for the film *The Chimney Sweep*

1958   Czechoslovak Peace Prize

LONDON FILM FESTIVAL: Special Honourable Mention for the film *The Lutchan War* (*The War Against the Lukanians* from *Old Czech Legends*)

1959   INTERNATIONAL FILM FESTIVAL, CANNES: Prize for the best national selection (*A midsummer Night's Dream, Longing, Butterflies Don't Live Here*)

1960   MONTEVIDEO FILM FESTIVAL: Second Prize in the puppet films class for the film *A Midsummer Night's Dream*

1961   BERGAMO: Gold Medal

1963   SAO PAULO: First Prize for costume designs for the play *Drahomíra* at the VII Biennale

BILBAO: Silver "Miqueldi" at the Fifth International Film Festival of Documentary film

Awarded the title National Artist in Czechoslovakia

INDEX